Ako-Aya
A Cameroonian Pioneer in Daring Journalism
Social Commentary (An Antology)

Patrick Tataw Obenson **1927-1979**

Ako-Aya
A Cameroonian Pioneer in Daring Journalism and Social Commentary
(An Anthology)

Ephraim N. Ngwafor

Langaa Research & Publishing CIG
Mankon, Bamenda

Publisher:
Langaa RPCIG
Langaa Research & Publishing Common Initiative Group
P.O. Box 902 Mankon
Bamenda
North West Region
Cameroon
Langaagrp@gmail.com
www.langaa-rpcig.net

Distributed outside N. America by African Books Collective
orders@africanbookscollective.com
www.africanbookscollective.com

Distributed in N. America by Michigan State University Press
msupress@msu.edu
www.msupress.msu.edu

ISBN: 9956-616-59-1

© Ephraim N. Ngwafor 2010
First published by Institute of Third World Art
& Literature, UK, 1989

DISCLAIMER

All views expressed in this publication are those of the author and do not necessarily reflect the views of Langaa RPCIG.

Content

Dedication vii

Introduction
The King is Dead 1

Chapter One
The Daring Nature of Ako-Aya 21

Chapter Two
Ako-Aya Against Tribalism 35

Chapter Three
Ako-Aya Exposes: The Vices of Certain House-Wives 45

Chapter Four
Ako-Aya and Prostitution 59

Chapter Five
Ako-Aya and Women from the East 73

Chapter Six
Ako-Aya and Women: Personal Experiences 79

Chapter Seven
Ako-Aya and Gossips 89

Chapter Eight
Ako-Aya and Letters to the Editor 101

Chapter Nine
Ako-Aya and his Enemies 105

Chapter Ten
Ako-Aya and the Big Towns 109

Chapter Eleven
Ako-Aya and Re-Unification 145

Chapter Twelve
Ako-Aya and Politics 155

Chapter Thirteen
Ako-Aya and the Big Stories 163

Chapter Fourteen
Ako-Aya's Problems at Job-Site 185

Chapter Fifteen
Ako-Aya and Misleading Titles 193

Chapter Sixteen
Ako-Aya and Christmas 201

Chapter Seventeen
Ako-Aya and the Fall of the City of Victoria 205

Chapter Eighteen
Ako-Aya and Fraud in the Bota Wharf 217

Chapter Nineteen
Ako-Aya - A Prophet of his Death 225

Chapter Twenty
Ako-Aya's Last Few Months on Earth 229

Epilogue 243

Dedication

TO MY FATHER

GIDEON ANYE ANGWAFOR

Introduction

The King is Dead

When, in 1952, King George VI of England died quietly in his sleep, the papers came out in the morning with identical headlines, "The King is Dead"; and when the rock star, Elvis Presley died in 1977 of a drug over-dose, papers all over the world, almost unanimously declared, "The King is Dead." Yes, there was no other fitting title to describe the death of Tataw Obenson on Sunday April 29th, 1979. "A King Died" in Victoria.

His death has created a big vacuum amongst our Cameroonian journalists. I read in him behaviour peculiar to both Martin Luther King, Jr., and Malcolm X, all of whom were freedom fighters in America; the only difference being that he hadn't the big degrees of Martin Luther King, Jr., or the war-like nature of Malcolm X. However, the trio preached justice. Again, in him, I saw a mind that is as rich as Jimmy Callaghan's and Winston Churchill's, all former Prime Ministers of England. What is more, like Jimmy Callaghan, he was a self-made intellectual who never acquired the work permits, (degrees), bestowed by academic institutions which have housed many of us for so long. Like Socrates and Plato, Tataw Obenson was a great teacher. Those who read his articles and never had their consciences sensitised, have been very hardened people indeed. We shall hardly have Tataw Obenson's double again amongst our journalists.

If there is one reason for writing this book, it is because I would like to see Tataw Obenson alive, and I doubt if there is any other way out than to produce his works in a more permanent form. To achieve this purpose, I have reminded myself of other publications such as Saint Paul's letter in the New Testament, Socrates' trial and several others which have been produced verbatim without any violence being done on any word, so as to maintain their authenticity.

Although Tataw Obenson wrote mainly in satires, their interpretations were as easy as being able to know that George Orwell was referring to Trotsky when he gave him a new name of Snowball in his well-known book, Animal Farm. To achieve his aim, he assumed a new name, *AKO-AYA*, by which he was known until his death. In fact, many people never even knew his true name. With his pen he fought for the common man, and in his attempt to stamp out fraud, bribery, and many other evils in our society, he caused many people in high offices to be on the alert. Whatever anybody did, he made sure AKO-AYA was not around. Small wonder that in the article below, he said as early as in 1971 that he was not unaware of the fact that many people would like to see him dead. He wrote on 10th February, 1971.

"WELL

"I came back Sunday looking very healthy and looking very fit. I thank those who contributed morally and financially to make me well. Especially, I thank A.L.A. of Buea, Monica and Lydia of Mamfe and George of Kumba. They had really sustained me where others failed. I thank still those who wanted me to die, notably FGD and CA of Victoria and several others in Buea, their names too scared to mention.

"So I went to OKU right there in the creature lake and this medicine man took me in a small canoe and asked me to confess my sins before he could give me the drug that will make me well. Well, what sins did I not confess - everything under the sun from murder to adultery, from nepotism to tribalism especially; on tribalism the medicine man was very severe, but I begged and promised that henceforth I would be an African first and that to me all Africans are the same no matter whether they are white, black or green, and especially that all Cameroonians from Garoua to Nkambe are the same and tribe now means nothing whether Manyu, Mooio, Mantung and Donga and Meme. He then pushed me into the lake and I swam to the shore feeling well except for my fingers.

"In the sea-port city, J was taking my usual afternoon stroll when a house-wife was spitting out pepper against her husband.

"The husband had merely done what every good Cameroon husband should do, that of marrying an additional wife. A mob of jeering school children was following her as she moved to the second wife's house, smashed everything including the girl's wig. I hear the second marriage must still take place.

"But back to Oku, many other people besides me go there: - there were football team managers, businessmen, Football Pools managers all seeking ways and means of getting rich quick. In fact, the Pools Manager was looking for some 'Mungang' that would make everybody stake only in his Pools. The football Manager wanted that there should be all in front of his goal mouth.

"Well, now that I have returned, I intend crawling to our high-society sport and surely will bring you in the next issue."

this is the style this great author employed. In one article, he could carry over ten messages. As you must have noticed in the above article, he talked of the following issues: those who would love to see him dead, tribalism, supernatural powers, women, and his ill-health, thus explaining why in several other articles which I will be discussing, he often talked of his trips to Oku.

Many political scientists would criticise a One-Party System as being undemocratic, but I could have sworn that AKO-AYA alone constituted a second party - The Opposition. He was the best watch-dog of his era. Highly unperturbed by court actions or arrests, he spoke out his mind, if only justice was attained, especially for the common man. Indeed, he was in detention in Buea when his beloved mother died. And when he was dragged to court for defaming the Cultural Delegate of West Cameroon, in 1972, AKO-AYA stood his ground. And this case stemmed from his allegation that the Cultural Delegate had received a bribe from people who were seeking licences to open new schools. The portion of his virile article read thus:

Everywhere I went in this town people talked about "Nothing but this new college without a site. Boh I hear for Radio say Mr. Thomas I college I dong get approval. I thought I heard that a certain big man in Buea announced after he took over office that no new school should operate this year. I saw the Land rover which St. Thomas had from Buea. I always like to mind my own business unless I see something bad that might affect the smooth running of our country."

"Something bad that might affect the smooth running of our country" always kept him worried and thus caused him to react - what an eminent Opposition Party he constituted himself.

When Ako-Aya died, a deep sense of loss gripped the Cameroonian people. Of all the tributes which were paid to him, two moved me and I think it was a great job done by these two people. The first article was a poem by one Mr. Samuel Mbella of the Theological College Nyasoso. On June 19th, 1979, he wrote in the Cameroon Outlook thus:

"That you have really gone
Is what remains to some of us
A mystery that tongue cannot tell.
That you have really gone
makes some of us to ask
How the Cameroon Outlook is going to look out

"That you have really gone
gives some of the chance to
violate some of your decrees
and rejoice but mourn cunningly
because we shall start all over again.

"That you have really gone
Makes us to ask the question
But who is the next bold journalist
To speak out what he sees?

Introduction: The King is dead

"Oh that you were still around
Would have been better
Your decrees are going to be violated
'Do not drink when driving and do not
drive when drinking.'

That you have really gone
Gives room to 'brife' and 'contrifashion'
Bribery and corruption
A thing you cried out against.
"Those who felt uneasy when you appeared
Should we say they are relieved
Because they have to start all over again.

"That you have really gone
Is a question worth asking
You who did not conceal anything
Made us to know by tricks
Those who took our wives and
Also our daughters in our absence.

"That you have really gone
Is true but untrue because
As one man puts it, 'a teacher never dies'
So, you are ever in our memories.

"That you have really gone
Is obvious and true
But one thing remains
You have left us for now and not for ever
So we shall surely meet again
Oh! with tears we say
MAY YOU REST IN PERFECT PEACE.

It was not only from the world of poetry that a telling dedication could be made to this hero, but Lawyer Asonganyi ably represented those who preferred to do so by prose. Thus, in an article "He was a Jeremy of a Decaying Social Order ", Lawyer Asonganyi, in typical style, wrote out a message which told you all: I adored and will always adore this article. (This came out on 19th May, 1979). He wrote:

"TRIBUTE TO A MARTYR

"He came to his own
And his own received him not;
But few that harkened his voice
Live to achieve his mission.

"Patrick Tataw Obenson was the Jeremy of a decaying social order that was not only deaf" to his lamentation but treated him as a traitor to its cause. Being a versatile voice in the wilderness some of his hearers called hira a fighter for the freedom of the press. Some the advocate of the liberties of man in a free society some a sarcastic and controversial critic, some the leader of the disgruntled elements in society, some a fault-finder of the wounded lion type, while the brain-washed treated him as a mad dog that ought to be chained and destroyed.

"But the fact was that Paddy was too much a realist for the materialistic mind to know and understand accurately. A victim of human suffering which he felt very keenly he devoted his short but extremely active life to airing his society of abnormal suffering otherwise known as outrageous injustice. As a close friend in joy and in sorrow I saw him take the ordinary sufferings of man as the tolls and taxes which man must pay in order to live the human life. He was therefore. a war of attrition against abnormal suffering or suffering intentionally created by man acting as a wolf to his fellow man in his devouring or the common wealth which his creator made for him and all the other mundane creatures. Much of the stuff of which he was made is seen vividly in one of his burning editorials entitled JUSTICE DELAYED (Cameroon Outlook, Friday 10th September 1976). It bears external testimony that Paddy was always up in arms against abnormal suffering no matter whatever he came across in his society.

"In this vein he lived; in it he developed high blood pressure when he saw that his simple life and fearless public denunciations of all that was evil in his society, instead of cleaning it up, only moved it to trample upon them and use them to harass and create more enemies against him; in it he finally died alone in a silence and in obscurity without wife and child, friend or foe, medical or red-cross officer, journalist or minister of religion in attendance by his death-bed.

"He died a hero in a class of his own stage as the chief character of a tragedy in which he had committed his audience to his cause that must be won. For, though his body lies moulding in his grave, his spirit goes matching on leading his army of crusaders to victory against the ills of the society that bore him.
"Long Live Patrick Tataw Obenson's spirit and crusade. Soonest may his dream come true."

I would highly agree with Lawyer Asongany, that the late Tataw Obenson was a martyr. Very few people would ever attempt to be as daring as he was. What impressed many was the fact that his cries were ever so often directed to the cure of evils against defenceless people. Thus, he did not only pass through his Ako-Aya column to express himself but also did so directly, via his Editorials. An example is the Editorial he wrote, entitled "The Increased Transport Fares", one month before his death. He declared that:

"Motor transport - the form of transport mostly used by the common people of this country has had its fares hiked from 5 to 6.5 francs per kilometre. This agreement has been reached between the transport union known as SETRACAUCAM and the Ministry of Transport.

"But is this increase really necessary? This transport union or its agents are already charging about 17.5 frs per kilometre and in the North West Province the charges are 25 frs per kilometre. The slight increase by the transport Ministry will only strengthen the hands of SETRACAUCAM to charge on its own even higher rates.

"The Cameroon Outlook views these increased fares exacted from the travelling public as an attempt by an agency to strangle the very people it is paid to protect - at least financially and calls on the heads of the different adminis-trative units to see that only the approved fares are paid.

"We further call on the public not to be silently oppressed people by SETRACAUCAM any more and to pay only the approved fares."

Who would not consider such an advice to the masses subversive? Yet Tataw Obenson marched on. Unfortunately, he could not live for long to continue his good works. He was a patient for a long time before his death. And he always reminded us in his Ako-Aya column of his ill-health. In fact, as early as 1971, he informed us of his regular visits to his doctor's. This is how he brought home this worrying part of his life.

AKO-AYA ON DANGER LIST

2nd February, 1971

"Well readers, I am afraid I will have to stop writing in this column soon as that dreadful disease doesn't want to give me any breathing space.

"Remember, I told you in the last issue to keep your fingers crossed? Yes, today, I say start praying for me, because my native doctor in Kumba says I am on the danger list.

"At Kumba, after- the small party at Olympic, I visited one of those herbal specialists. I mean the native doctor at Hausa Quarters and told him what is worrying me.

Introduction: The King is dead

"Would you believe it readers, that this man asked me to give him one goat, a cock, a bottle of whisky (even though he drinks matutu), and five thousand francs as consultation fees. "Poor me, I had only my transport fare of four hundred francs to carry me from Kumba to Victoria. All my money had been stolen at 'Big-mot' market at Hausa Quarters by pick-pockets who throng the area, but playing 'the Gentleman' I did not raise an alarm. That would have been of little use because in flocking round me even my shoes would have been stolen from my feet if I had raised a cry over the money.

"No back to my native doctor. I told him to let me go to the bank, and stopping a township taxi, I rushed in and ordered the driver to take me to Mbonge road.
"When he got there I told him to let me greet somebody and passing besides one house I ran behind a dozen other houses and entered my aunt's room from back.

"The driver got tired of waiting for me and after sounding his horn for a full half hour he gave up the fifty francs and drove off. My aunt gave me 10.000 francs to pay for my treatment and making off straight for the native Doctor I paid him for the goat, the cock and the sum required.

"The man asked me to undress, then told me a long story about witches who were after my life. As for my treatment he told me to sit in the sun for four hours every day for two days. "Readers, I have been sitting in the sun for the past five days only to hear that I might die of the disease.

"I hear there is a better native Doctor up North at a place they called Oku. If there is still any life left in me by tomorrow I shall hurry up there and gamble for my life. But I need some donations to pay my way. Over to you readers. "I promise you very interesting stories when

I get well again."

Struggling on, Tataw Obenson decided to visit the native doctor in Oku, if only they would save his life. That he was really in pains, caused him to write three articles in three immediate publications. It should be recalled that even before the above article, he had already alluded to his illness in a preceding article of 28th January, 1971, entitled, "IN KUMBA", in which he asked his readers to keep their fingers crossed. Thus, unmindful of the fact he ran the risk of boring his readers with one topic in three articles, Ako-Aya still felt it necessary to inform his sympathisers in a third article on 5th February, 1971:

"STOP-OVER IN BAMENDA DURING MY WAY TO OKU

"I received the following telegram this morning at the Highland Hotel and it speaks for itself, Ako-Aya: DONATIONS to the 'AKO-AYA's get-well fund' continue to raise latest donors are DTA of Buea stop, Land rover instructed proceed to your destination.

"Publisher - Outlook

"I have been here for a couple of days, having been brought up by the grace of this time of another chief. Sometimes when death is near it is good to take stock of what we have done on earth; after all the creator will not seek thy grace. You may be white or black. He will not seek thy birth, you may be a wretch like myself or the President of the greatest country in the world what he demands is 'what have you done on earth. So I thought of all the good I have done and there was precious little and I thought of the evil I have done and there was much -~ my ungratefulness for kindness done, the new meaning I have given to the word, 'Subversive', the several, journalists I got imprisoned and detained, the frigidaires I bought for girlfriends, the several homes

I had broken by alienating the feelings of the wives and oh so much more evil, the tribalism I preach against and yet practice and I went down on my knees asking everybody that the creator gives me a few days longer that I may turn over a new leaf, that I may use every bit of me to help my fellow men.

"This chief came and bundled me into his car. In fact I was put into the boot, what with all the grime on me and we travelled from my 'bush' hospital to Kumba and thence to Bamenda without food. The chief seems to be made of stone - not wanting food or drinks.

"Everybody from down-south is in Bamenda, because the As-sizes you know, the usual crowd most of them flashing their new cars, their advantage from the misfortune of those people who wanted to declare war on their fatherland. "I was the only other guest of the Highland and I made straight away for my room and blessed sleep stole over me, till I was woken by the room steward saying a girl had come to the hotel ... I dragged my sick-self to the drinks and I saw her - five foot twenty stone bulk of foo-foo corn and Achu. Orange was her choice but she didn't refuse a dash of whisky into the orange. It was too early to go to bed, but she said that she would come back later. 'That afternoon there had been these up:- North Society weddings in Tamuluh Baptist Church she had confided in me when she came back later and the biting cold now does not permit anybody sleeping alone, no wonder the teaming population.

"The morning brought its difficulties - 'give me money I go now' she kept on repeating. I dipped my hands several times into my pocket knowing that there was no money there and told her to go first j no sooner did 7 have occasion to leave the room that it was locked and she took the keys away also my glasses.

"I took all the forces of a turbaned journalist up North and traced her and got back the key. The other nights have found me lying down on my sick bed.

"Tomorrow, if the land rover comes I leave for OKU, I will surely right from there if this ghastly malaria does not take me to the land of no return. I thank those who have contributed to my get well fund and dead or alive I will not forget them."

Note that Ako-Aya talks of malaria instead of high blood pressure. I think he felt it unnecessary to tell us everything. This is what killed him nine years after these first publications.

WHO WAS TATAW OBENSON ALIAS AKO-AYA?

When Ako-Aya died in 1979, I was still in London working towards my Ph.D. thesis on Insurance Law. Thus, my only account of his death was the various versions I got from his friends who were in Victoria, at the time of his death. I have decided not to rely on such hearsay evidence; instead, I went over to Bota to talk to his best friend, Wem Muambo, in whose presence one of our finest journalists died. From him, I did not only uncover the manner in which he died but also what pre-occupied his mind the last few days before his death.

In 1927, a male child was born to an Ossing family based in Etchi-Njock in Manyu Division, and it was agreed that he be called Patrick Tataw Obenson. When he became of age his parents sent him to a Government Primary School in Kumba and later on in Basseng. At the end of a successful stay in these institutions, he was admitted into Sasse College, which institution outdistanced and still outdistances our numerous colleges in popularity.

Like it was in those days, big companies scrambled for those young men who left Sasse College, and it was as a result of this advantage that Patrick Tataw Obenson got his first gainful employment with Plantations Pamol du Cameroun. After several shuttles to Nigeria and back, this hero to-be finally settled on Journalism, first as a broadcaster with Radio Cameroon and later as a newspaper man.

Introduction: The King is dead

Tataw Obenson was the brain, indeed, the architect of the very popular programme 'Where are We?' during his stay in Radio Cameroon. Through this medium, the ordinary man was able to express his worries and dissatisfaction, with a result that many social and economic improvements were effected. Sadly enough, this programme soon disappeared into thin air.

Maybe out of anger, Obenson decided to enter a new club of newspaper journal ism. In this vein, his first attachment was with the CAMEROON STAR, printed in Mutengene by Hope Printing Press. Again, being a man of the people, he triggered off a war between himself and the Law Enforcement Bureau, as a result of his heart breaking editorials. Small wonder that he served a nine months detention for advocating in one of such editorials for the immediate dismissal of the Chief Executive Officer of the then West Cameroon government. Indeed, he had to be escorted from his cell to his late mother's corpse. When the Cameroon Star went into liquidation, he tried his hand again this time in partnership with Mr. Samuel Peter Liga, both of whom founded the Cameroon Telegraph. But the partnership soon flopped as a result of constant disagreement between the joint owners.

And this is how the Cameroon Outlook was born in the later part of 1969. Within, the founder saw an opportunity to carry out a mission, a mission with nobody stepping on his way, at least from within. He could now do his own thing. Assuming the column entitled Ako-Aya, (in one of his articles, 'From Kumba with Love' published in March, 1971, he made known the meaning of Ako-Aya, namely, "Let them take and cook"). Tataw Obenson spearheaded a moral crusade which was bent on achieving social, political, cultural and economic reforms. He saw in himself a prophet who came to sensitise the conscience of every superior officer with his popular advice, "Thou shalt not oppress the poor." And how he succeeded in stamping out many evils in our society. Yes, his progressive attitude he gave CAMEROON a new OUTLOOK.

It was, therefore, not surprising that when I met his best friend, Wem Muambo, sometime in June, 1981, that is, over two years after Obenson's death, we took over one hour for an interview which was scheduled for just 30 minutes. This was because I had to spend so much time consoling with my interviewee who could hardly make two successful sentences about his friend without weeping. He even confessed to me that he has asked Obenson's wife not to come to see him regularly, because such visits only come to remind him of a nightmare.

Wem Muambo, who is now attached to the Public Relations Department in the C.D.C., first met Tataw Obenson in 1962, when himself, Tataw Obenson and Achidi Diffang were absolved by Radio Cameroon. These three friends shared one bed; since salaries always delayed in going through, and being a correspondent for several newspapers, notably, 'Reuters', Wem was able to keep all of them going. This is how Obenson became his life long friend. A trained journalist, Wem Muambo, in addition to his calling with the C.D.C., is also an agent for the Africa Magazine, and has been one since its inception. With this bond bridging them together, Wem Muambo had a big part to play when Obenson founded his new paper, Cameroon Outlook. Indeed, Wem's office was a mere extension of Obenson's; there, I was shown files of the different employees and those which were meant for other administrative improvements. Being an untrained journalist, Obenson relied so much on Wem who edited most of the articles for his friend. In fact, some of the Ako-Aya series like those on "DREAMS", which I will later refer to, were written by Wem.

Hence, it was not surprising that on the invitation of Tataw Obenson, a meeting was arranged for Sunday, 29th April, 1979, mainly to discuss the future of 'Cameroon Outlook'. Obenson's paper was in a crisis, and so he needed his friend badly to help solve problems of management. According to Wem, however, the main topic was that of the conduct of one of the workers (I won't release his name, since he now runs his own paper, for fear that it would jeopardise his business) who had been found to be incorrigibly corrupt. Wem claims that he had had to sustain this other journalist for about two years, because Obenson had since long wanted to dismiss him. At this point, Wem had also got to breaking point, and would without any hesitation on this 29th day of April, 1979, have voted in favour of the dismissal.

The meeting point was at their usual palm wine spot under a mango tree at Middle Farms, Wem was expecting him at 5 p.m. Obenson had earlier on in the morning made up his mind to attend the Sasse College come-together which was scheduled for that same day. However, he changed his mind and took off his well ironed suit.

His mistress Dora Ngembus (he had spent the night at her house in the CDC camp in Middle Farms), then asked him to accompany her to Tiko for some family matter, but he turned the invitation down and preferred to 'REST.' She, therefore, left alone. Obenson was left in the house with a small girl of about nine years. Suddenly he started sweating profusely. This frightened the small girl who did just the right thing, namely, alerting the neighbours with loud cries. By the time they arrived, Patrick Tataw Obenson, a king, was dead. He laid there on the bed as if sleeping. What a quiet way to say au revoir to your friends. He failed to keep to his rendezvous at 5 p.m.

When Wem got to the scene, (he also lives in Middle Farms), he quickly telephoned some of the Bayangi elements. He was totally confused and helpless. Yet he had to prove his manhood, fight a war against tears, nervousness and make the necessary arrangements for the conveyance of the corpse. Thus, he telephoned Lawyer Ebai, but unfortunately he was not in and thus, he passed on the message to Mrs. Ebai. For a woman, I am sure she must have been motionless. The next person to be contacted was Dr. Agbor While He Lived

Walter Stifter (Wearing Number 63): He was Champion in Three Straight Race, Shattering Myths & Creating Records in the Process

The Late Man (Second From Left) Waiting to Be Greeted by the Then Minister of Information and Culture Mr Vroumsia Tchinaye

I Ate Mr Obenson (Second from Right) at a Reception Given by Ethiopian Airlines in Addis Ababa

Introduction: The King is dead

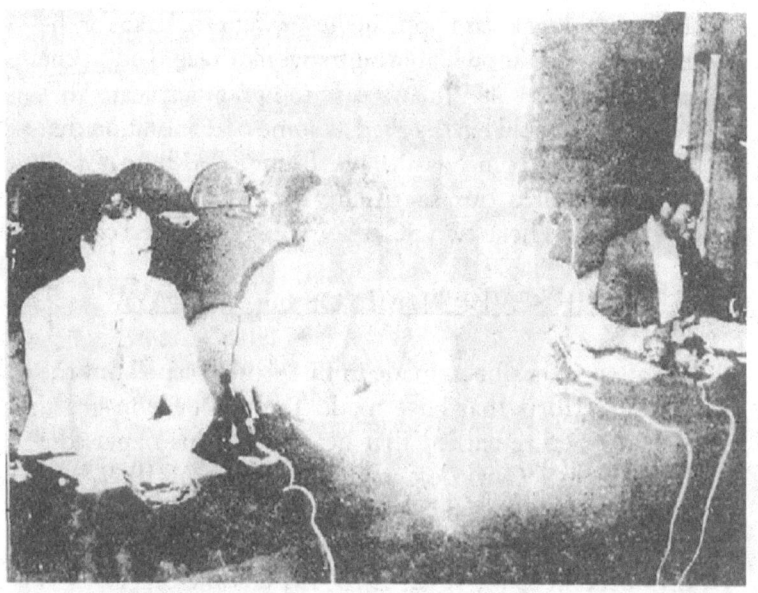

The Late Mr Obenson Listening Attentively During an Ipi Conference in Lagos

Since Wem did not want to face up to the disgrace of letting others know that his very good friend had died in the house of his mistress, he quickly arranged for 3 Peugeot pick-up owned by one Mr. Yonda and in it they were able to convey the mortal remains to his matrimonial home which was situated behind Bay Hotel. Unfortunately, the deceased's wife had travelled to Mamfe. To gain entry into the house, Wem had to break the door.

In the course of our conversation, I asked Wem to comment on the allegation that Obenson had joined a secret society which rules he had breached and so had to pay a price of death. With vehemence, Wem argued that this was not true, and explained it away with his assertion that Obenson, on the contrary, believed in having friends. I would leave you all, gentle readers, to picture for yourself the commotion and shock with which the Victoria population received the news.

For one thing, I was happy he never went to Sasse for the reunion; who knows, maybe he would have died in the campus as was late Quan's case the previous year. This, of course, would have served as some corroboration that those of us from Sasse have founded a 'juju house' which requires our sacrificing one of our members every year. These two SOBANS died of natural causes.

THE SEVERAL MINDS OF AKQ-AYA

An attempt has been made in this work to spell out the various efforts that have made Tataw Obenson great. It had .been remarked that he founded his paper, the 'Cameroon I Out took in the later part of 1969, and almost immediately; Ako-Aya was born. However, I have been selective, choosing mainly the articles he produced in 1971, 1972, 1973, 1974, some bits in 1976 and 1978, and also those he wrote a few j months before his death in 1979. In reading through these works, you will be able to discover the strength of this [satirist, and also be able to follow up the life in the city of Victoria in particular, and former West Cameroon in [general, from 1971 to 1979, when he died. His articles spoke it all.
In the various sub-heads that follow, the several minds of this great Professor-journalist have been exposed.

Introduction: The King is dead

*After a Hard Day's Work The Late Man Relaxes
with his Professional Colleagues*

*Late Pto Who Was a Very Good Mixer is Seen Announcing the Programme
during the Fako Mini-cultural Festival in the Jungle Village Victoria*

Obenson and Friend, Jerome Gwellem

Chapter One

The Daring Nature of Ako-Aya

Unmindful of all the consequences that could follow, Ako-Aya spoke out his mind whenever his sense of justice was offended. Thus, in condemning bribery and corruption, he exposed those Administrators who asked for ten percent of the profits of every contract given out, and also took to task those who received such compensation in kind, e.g., gifts of goats. The virile nature of this courageous journalist led him to spell out names without fear of a court action. This explains his war of letters with Chief Makoge.

In fact, it was Ako-Aya who questioned the government why there were such alarming delays in paying teachers in former West Cameroon. Yet, another event that springs to mind about the daring nature of this journalist is the article he wrote on the train accident which occurred in September 1976, between Yaounde and Douala. As the government attempted to hide the true figures of the dead and wounded, Ako-Aya came out with evidence that stunned everyone. Again, this was typical of him, he would unearth anything.

And like he did in his article of November 26, 1971, about the Prefect of Tiko, he never failed to give praise where praise was due.

(i) Herein are the relevant articles:

(i) <u>TUESDAY APRIL 6, 1971</u>:
<u>THIS TEN PERCENT DEAL</u>

"I know I should have been beaten up long before, but it was only over the week-end that some one came quite out in the open, rolled up his sleeves to beat me to pulp, but midair his hands stopped and the voice of reason prevailed. But I just wanted him to touch me and I would have shown him that 'one day Monkey go market i no go come back.'

"I promised on my mother's grave it's all about this ten percent deal. I do not know why dealers like ten, nobody wants five or nine percent, but I understand they hit on ten because it is easier to divide or multiply if you still remember your arithmetic rules. So it is easier to work out what ten percent of five million francs is and you can start figuring out what share you come in for and start thinking how you could well spend it.

"So this red man is head of a very big depart-ment, advertises for tenders for building a rest house, another big man is for building a hotel. Three contractors win the tender, one is to construct up to the floor, another up to wall plate, another to complete - just contractor and you get only ten percent but three contractors and you get three times ten percent. He gets his cut, it is said on the floor level, even the wall plate man reluctantly pays him but the third man is very clever. You know this Banyangi people they think they are very clever and he wants to pay only after he has collected his share through his bankers. Those are not the rules of the game you pay before the service is rendered as my girl friend says 'payment before service.'
"But I see only very little space has been allotted to me this issue and I am bound to stop."

(ii) <u>"FRIDAY JUNE 4, 1971
GOAT</u>

Goat-meat has become quite a delicacy these days instead of chicken. Thus the pubs and hotels now excel in goat Pepper-soup, goat and goat sawyer. In fact the demand is so great that Bolifamba, Muea and Kumba that used to be the source of supply have all dried up and Bamenda is now the source of supply.

"Dis I say Bamenda is the source of supply, Buea is also a source and the houses formerly occupied by expatriates in Buea now form the market.

Chapter One: The Daring Nature of Ako-Aya

"Of course I could never have known how these goats get to Buea till a friend told me they order from Bamenda. "Well let us begin by the fact that they are always a dash from poor farmers up North to this big man from down south; of course a special vehicle came up empty in order to return to the Coast with this type of gift. You know these types of vehicles with green, red and yellow stripes, yours and ray tax helped to buy,

"These goat farmers who find it hard to keep soul and body together will let them not give this dash of a goat and none of their requests will be granted. Then on your and my petrol the goats reach Buea. The house-boy becomes middle-man for the goat transaction and the goat-sawyer man runs up. Sometimes as much as five thousand francs exchanged hands for one goat. "Well, the money - it only goes to keep the girl-friends more comfortable.

"Others rear theirs, and the goat dung virtually litters these houses white men occupied. They will be sold near Christmas at thrice their price.

"Perhaps when next I visit Bamenda, I will bring my own dash of goat. But the fun of it all is that because it is high, I must obtain a certificate from the Veterinary Department and very heavily for taxi."

(iii) <u>"WEDNESDAY JUNE 2, 1971;</u>
<u>SPECIALLY FOR CHIEF MAKOGE</u>

"When I wrote about 'I won't leave' in this paper of 19th May 1971, I hadn't chief Makoge in mind. I remember in 1964 when the chief was celebrating his 60th birthday, he insulted a neighbour's wife and threw whisky at a colleague. Today chief Makoge's age stands at 58 a form of geometrical unprogression. "The chief has opened a broadside on me which I will allow readers to judge for themselves. Readers should note the very wrong spelling of words, obviously expected of a man who barely reached class four, whose colleagues have all retired from the service, and who grows younger everyday.

"I like to respect age and hardly like writing this but then the chief has brought it all on himself. Chief Makoge should make way for young men to take over his place. In the faces of employment, is it correct to keep men who have hit eighty?

"Now read chief Makoge's trash which is incoherent and merely a jumble of words.

"Dear Sir,

"'Please allow me space in your widely read paper to make a brief observation on the article captioned I won't leave" published in the 'AKO-AYA' column of the Cameroon Outlook of 19th May, 1971.

"'Apart from the article being incoherent and illogical, I note very disappointedly that the columnist "Ako-Aya displays journalistic incompetence and thereby repudiates the standard Free Lance Journalism in Cameroon. Take a classical example of his article "I won't leave" in which he struggled to correlate the unwilling-ness of some employees to accept obnoxious decisions and to leave Government or Corporation service with a completely domestic affair as a woman refusing to leave her husband's house. Maybe, marriages in the area where AKO-AYA hails from are contracted so ordinary short term employment contract.'

"Let's examine along with my readers an extract of the same article which reads:

Chapter One: The Daring Nature of Ako-Aya

"'You remember one of these many Buea based Chiefs who started working before my mother was born and now count their years backwards - well he has said "I won't go" and has stayed put.'

"'Let us leave the question discussing "work" or "career" which AKO-AYA may not have success-fully carried out and consider one simple point in this statement. It is a custom in Africa that men claim their fathers whereas women claim their mothers.

"Although we may doubt "AKO-AYA's" sex, it would be unfortunate if that name were borne by a man as the maternal inclination which has portrayed in his statement ... started work before my mother was born ..." certainly suggests that he is one of those born by an unknown fathers.

"The public looks forward to our local journalists to show a high sense of duty and prove themselves as Cameroonians capable of meeting with any international challenge in a prominent profession such as Journalism. On the other hand, it becomes very unpalatable for journalists, of the standard and morale of 'AKQ-AYA' who, perhaps out of a depression of personal failures in life, frustration and professional incompetence, degenerate into a state of journalism which is calumnious and unprogressive.

"This situation of things was what certainly led a prominent Defence Counsel to term the journalistic conduct of one of our citizens in court as struggling and staggering.

"Chief (Nhon) O.N. MAKOGE,
Buea: 25-5-1971."

(iv) **"WEDNESDAY JUNE 16, 1971:
MY LETTER FROM CHIEF MAKOGE**

"Dear Ako-AYA,

"I wish to issue a rejoinder to the article entitled 'SPECIAL FOR CHIEF MAKOGE' which appeared in the AKO-AYA column of the Outlook of 2nd June, 1971. In that article and in the usual manner of his marginal thinking 'AKO-AYA' raised comments of dissimilative facts. He started his defence by stating "when I wrote about 'I won't leave' in this paper of the 19th May, 1971, I hadn't Chief Makoge in mind" but because statements of lies can never be defended for long, he soon made his conscience to be understood by stating further 'Chief Makoge should make way for young men to take over the place.' Without adding anything further on this point, it is left to readers to access the mentality and writing standard of a journalist of the type of 'AKO-AYA' who tried to palliate his poor standard of journalism by telling readers to note 'the very way wrong spelling of words' which did not exist in my article.

"'It is an undeniable truth that because of the lack of interesting news items and in order to dissipate the state of pecuniary embarrassment into which he has been perpetually thrown, 'AKO-AYA' invents false stories which aimed at assassinating the character of well-meaning persons, merely to enable his paper sell. For example, he tried to make readers to believe that in 1964 I celebrated my 60th birthday.

"AKO-AYA had never been an intelligent civil servant before he was dismissed with ignominy, he would have recalled that by 1964, the age for retirement was 60 and Government could not have kept someone who was a celebrant of that age.

Chapter One: The Daring Nature of Ako-Aya

"'Again, to reveal the journalistic hoax to which he has become an irretrievable victim, AKO-AYA further tells readers that I insulted a neighbour's wife and threw whisky at her colleague during the birthday celebration. The fact that - such scandalous acts were known to no other person else than AKO-AYA who was perhaps the lone invitee to the celebrations, reveals the deceptive role which this journalist has been playing through his publication.

"I do not know what AKO-AYA has in mind when he described me in his article as a man "who grows younger every day."

"'Age, it is said, is a matter of feeling and not of years. I do not know AKO-AYA's age. He may be a young man of thirties but I want him to note that there are young men of his age who look older than persons of eighty. The reason for this may not only be attributable to their progeny but also to the deplorable standards of living of such young men. Certainly filth, poor meals and disease do not give people their natural looks. In fact I know of a young man in Victoria who is as young as "Ako-Aya but who, because he is always filthy and leaves on poor meals, is so badly diseased and deformed that he does only look as a man of age of ninety but finds it difficult to wear trousers, shoes, ties and other apparels which move the pride of other young men - what an unfortunate position for that young man'
"Ms I do not wait to distract the attention of my readers from the topic which forms the main reason of this article, I wish to advise that AKO-AYA should improve on the standard of this journalism. It does not pay to pride in the publication of false and incriminating stories. 'PRIDE GOES BEFORE DESTRUCTION'.

"Finally, my challenge to the journalistic ability of AKO-AYA is that this article be published in full with his further observations which I will happily read.

"Yours faithfully,

"Chief (Nhon) O.N. Makoge

"Dear Chief,

"I have accepted your challenge and published your story, could you also accept my own challenge and resign in order to make room for young men.

"Honest you are 80 years old."

(v)   "TUESDAY JUNE 8, 1971: DETAINED

"If a school teacher in Kumba ask you to sit down and have a drink, please if you have no money on you, don't. This was the situation I found myself last Saturday when a college friend turned teacher invited me out. He left after he had downed 3.5 bottles of Cold Hearts as opposed to my 1.5 especial and I ended in paying for 5. "Chiefs welcome me and even this newly appointed big man settled me in for Brandy and Ginger at the Authentique.

"Came Sunday and we are all coming after an all night meeting. The usual stop check for travelling papers went on every ten miles till we got to Muyuka at 11.30 on Sunday the year of our Lord 1971, 6th June.

"This time not only were we to show our identity cards but party and voter's cards. A Nigerian was asked to come down from the vehicle because he had no party card despite the fact that he showed his pass-port. Only indigenes hold party cards. Came my turn and I politely told the man that only the president of my cell or party official could ask to see my card, as for my voter's card I told him that the voters card expressly says that "this card may be handed in for safe custody at the Prefecture after voting." I showed him my "Identity" card and Laissez-Passer.

Chapter One: The Daring Nature of Ako-Aya

"He turned and raged because I had politely challenged his authority and said till I show my party card and voter's card I was not moving.

"His comrade came. I sat quietly as the vehicle had gone leaving me behind. This comrade recognised me and asked the matter. With exaggerations he explained and the two spoke something quietly. They then allowed me go.

"This is the way things are and the way things will be but 'I shall not waste my days in trying to prolong them, I shall use my time'.

"If you must travel past Muyuka do not fail to carry your Identity card, Laissez-Passer, Party card, Voters card, certificates of fitness and conviction and your passbook."

(vii)   "TUESDAY OCTOBER 12, 1971:
JAM PAS DIE DEM HOLD ME FOR AIRPORT

"I missed my plane to Yaounde by a few minutes and stranded together with some two Anglophone friends I just made at the Douala airport, we decided to reach the 'gare' for this bad luck train.

"They hurriedly bought first class tickets and but for my kontri man we de work for hanya road I should have followed suit. My friends are now resting in peace.

"Massa no bi blood this, I saw agony and death and I marvelled. There were cries all over the whole forest. Police, civilians, red cap men, soldiers, everybody cried. Some for losing their libs, some in fear and some for just because friends were mangled to eternity. Well, majunga has taken its toll. Cameroonians know nothing as well as the cup. That's where the cup has landed hundreds of Cameroonians.

"Our laisez-faire is getting to extremes that have begun taking lives.

"And so I arrived back to the expenditure. I thought many friends would see me and be happy I am back alive. But alas they continued pouring in to the house 'Beau we hear you are a survivor. Pass some thing now.'

"In that way, I ran out my pockets and I am at the point of not even coming to work. No umbrella, no money and there are the rains. That's the way Cameroonians condole with their brethren."

(vii)   "TUESDAY OCTOBER 12, 1971:
JAM PAS DIE DEM HOLD ME FOR AIRPORT

"I fear guns more than anything else in my life and when I looked around the Douala airport and saw just guns with hardly any visible people behind them since the pillars as they appeared to me at first stood so erect I started shivering like jelly-fish, struggling hard to stop the urine which forcefully trickled down, soiling my already worn out suit. I jumped when one of what I thought to be pillars stamped his foot angrily and shouted ' Arrest Ako-Aya.'
"I opened my eyes and found myself lying on my hard plank bed.

"The stamping of the foot was all part of a dream, but some one was knocking on the door. It was Monday, the day I was supposed to follow my publisher to Ethiopia and the man who knocked handed my passport.

"I stayed back to accumulate some current Material from Cameroon to leave behind before proceeding to meet my master. I would have left everything to my assistant, but how could I when so many things are overtaking me so fast.

Chapter One: The Daring Nature of Ako-Aya

"I am not talking about this top secretary in one of these our big offices in Bota who nearly beat up our hefty Chef de Publicite for telling the world that she wears the mini.

"Apparently she is the only woman in Cameroon who still advocates the 'Caba.' I am not even writing about this beauty attached to this big money house in Victoria who decided to share a boy-friend with her bosom friend working in this big car company near the Victoria round about.

"I hear this up station journalist is threaten-ing to write me a stinker because I said he sold his sister to me for 400 francs. 'That's how the world goes these days. You tell a simple truth and all you get is a summons. 'This week there will be a series of parties and I am sorry I have to miss all these since I will be in Ethiopia.

"All the same, I have to cry that Outlook music fanatic and the rest of them to rock it out when Bay Hotel opens her new Saloon including Eddy, the Cameraman without a studio.

"The New Town furniture boss will also throw a party at Miramare Hotel after talking to the Press and the Guinness people are sending yet another invitation for the visit of one of their directors who will be received at the Buea Mountain Hotel.
"If you ever think of throwing a party, don't restrict these young struggling journalists in Victoria because by letting them into your party you will be helping them to help your self.
"See next issue."

(viii) **"FRIDAY NOVEMBER 26,1971: MASSA PLIFE, WE TENK YOU**

"Today I have written about two burning issues. Before you read them, say a prayer for me, perhaps I may not be living by the next issue. And now for (1) MASSA PLIFE, WE TENK YOU. "When a few weeks ago I started hammering at Tiko, it was to get the Authorities to act and they have acted well and quickly. By clarification of the Prefectorial Order, Taxis can operate between Victoria, Tiko, Buea and Muyuka from dawn to dusk, that is for 24 hours, without anybody standing by the way side to take their numbers and make them pay either to Government or to agencies. People will now be able to show in Tiko for a long time and be sure of transport to Buea or Victoria and economic life in Tiko will improve.

"It is rarely that I praise a Government official for doing his work for which my meagre tax pays him but I have to thank his life for listening to my complaints on behalf of the people.
"I realise many people will lose revenue especially in Tiko by this clarification.

"In fact Tiko changed this simple P. order in to a curfew. I hear their demands from Girl friends for Xmas can no longer be met as the extra money is not forth-coming and they can no longer keep their army of leg-men to look for women and collect money from Taxi Drivers, so they are disbanding.

ANO WAN GO FURTHER STUDIES

"Time it was when it was the yearning of civil servants to either go on study leave or Technical Aid to improve himself in his work, and thus become more efficient, gain promotion and increase one's earnings.

Chapter One: The Daring Nature of Ako-Aya

"But the manoeuvres of one of these capital Bees makes some of us fear, to even go on leave not to talk of going Overseas. They know what vacancies will exist where five years from hence. If it is too glaring to send some dollars overseas from the West, they for no reason transfer him to Douala or Yaounde and from there, away for further studies. Do not forget these big Bees have their men all over. From there away from the limelight he goes abroad to do one course or the other and returns.

"Should a high post be held by a lesser Bee, for no reason he is sent either on leave or even if he didn't apply goes for technical Aid. One's place is soon filled by another and on the return you have to take your queue and maybe suffer unemployment for several months.

"Look around Kumba the same process goes on, not to talk of Victoria or Buea where the process goes on surely but with relentless fury."

*Obenson (Third From Right) During a Visit
to the Ycb Brewery in Douala*

Chapter Two

Ako-Aya Against Tribalism

Ako-Aya spared no effort to discourage tribalism. This explains the purport of his very leading article 'The Four Bees', whereby he sought to expose and thus put an end to, the tribalistic tendencies of the Bansos, Bametas, Banyangis and Bakossis. It was this spirit of oneness that pushed him to write the article "Speaking From My Heart", in which he invited the people of Victoria to discard private interests and go in for a club merger. This he felt was the only mechanism through which Victoria could be represented in the Premier Football League. That he was right can be seen from the fact that seventeen years later, Victoria has not yet been able to produce such a team.

Ako-Aya's objective progressive nature cannot be doubted. It is interesting to note the sort of remarks he personally made about the Manyu people. Small wonder that when he too was attacked for being tribalistic, he had to work hard, like the first two articles below show, to explain to the people that this allegation was untrue.

i) "JANUARY 21,1976: PLEASE EXCUSE ME

"Yes please excuse me. Excuse me to ask why some women keep their fattest afro wigs to wear them at night when attending films. Two of us were sitting just behind such a lady once last Saturday and we had to bend all the time in order to just peep.

"Yes excuse me, but last month African Federation of Journalists (A.F.J.) wanted all big journalists to attend this very meeting about Press Freedom never won on a platter of gold, but bear with me and excuse me whether it was fear or what, but I did not attend. Yes excuse me I was not afraid of any plane crash, you see they say I do not write this column very well, yes excuse me they say I have remained at it too long, excuse me they accuse me of tribalism and all isms-ships you can think of just excuse we but I did not attend.'Where is this great columnist from Cameroon,' my colleagues asked but please excuse me I did not attend.

"Why don't you excuse me to pose just another question which is better to get, a permanent girl-friend or a kick and pass. They say just like comprehensive insurances dem dear so with permanent g.f.'s Dem say yes excuse me kick and pass no di loss plenty money. Well, excuse me which is better?"

ii) "MARCH 10, 1976: MONEY PLENTY: MIMBO FINISH BAYANGI GO DIE ALL"

"I am all sure you have met them before. Who you may ask, who else but this couple who cash in on human frailties. The story goes that for market day massa did send madam for go find chop money. They have an only 12-year-old daughter who in six months has been put in the family way by ten different people, who have paid through their nose to avoid going to court.

"The couple dem get money plenty, they are even building a zinc house, yet but money at what price?
"I do not just know what most tribes find in drinks. Like these Manyu tribes. They tend to behave as if its drinks that they breathe. So I was in this death celebration place.

"As each franc fell names entered the register. Then came the drinks and it was a roll call. Within a short time the queue was wonderful. Shouts came from all parts of the Joint. Impersonation and all the like.

"One man whose name is Ako Aya impersonated for Ako-Aya and took my own bottle. Mimbo slaves took to fighting. It was such a disgraceful sight. But that's what mimbo means to Manyu people.

"One other day there was this black clothe removal at church street, it was the same thing.

"Others had to be carried on stretchers to their houses and still others are in hospital. "Just around there I heard people whispering: 'Sign a decree now that there should be no mimbo and there will be no Manyu Division because all Bayangi people will die.' That's it. Its the new way of life.

"I do not want to talk about these girls nowadays who love boys now for seka money. The other day I saw some of these girls trying to fight for my sake, 'I no sabi if na dem bi talk say make my mother born me I fine', to love is to spend."

iii)   'WEDNESDAY SEPT.7, 1971: THE
               FOUR BEES

"Banso, Bameta, Bayangi and Bakossi these are the four 'Bees' that form this part of the Federation. I have chosen on them not because they are an intelligent minority as some of them claim, but because if there are any tribesmen so tribalistic that they tend to defeat the doctrine of oneness preached by our great party it is members of these tribes.

"I peeped at the last list of those who benefitted from Technical Aid - almost every body comes from the four 'Bees.' I looked at those who gain scholarships just one tribe. I looked at our Secretary Generals the majority are from these tribes. What of the Principals of Presbyterian schools most from one tribe, and then who is sewing nurses' uniforms in the entire Federation this one woman from this tribe.

"And then I am surprised when I hear them, mount the soap-box but one learns to be surprised at nothing. Not when an Engineer last Saturday if rubbing grease on one's body makes one an Engineer, drank so much in Limbe River Club and as my little son said 'i shit for his trouser' and the feaces entered the cushions and he was lifted with all that filth into his car an expatriate for that matter.

"Again how can I be surprised when persons who have cases pending in court are making frantic efforts through former girl-friends to save their skins. These days I am really surprised at nothing. This is the way things are and the way they will be."

iv) <u>"FRIDAY SEPT.10, 1971: MY MAIL</u>

"Before I continue further to discuss my mail, I like to thank the people of this paper for coming up very often during the past fortnight. I suppose they are aiming at a daily paper, in that case I like advertisers to help make the 'Outlook' a daily, they would be helping them-selves tremendously.
"But lest the Editor would be feeling proud, I like to tell him that there is still more room for improvement.

"Well, there is the letter that landed on my desk this morning:

"'My Dear Nkwane Ako-Aya,

"'Your publications are most interesting and real - eye opener, but while you do this, I like you always to make a careful study of a situation before you report because you are likely to give a false impression to the public.

"Ako-Aya, take the recent case of the 'Four Bees' as you reported. I am sure that you were not vigilant enough else you should have seen these other 'Bees' in the Judiciary and in the police too.

"But, dear Ako-Aya are there any Bees that do not merit their positions? If so give them the impression that there is no tribalism.

"After all, Ako-Aya even your 'Four Bees' are spotted over the West sector of Cameroon and it is no fault of theirs that they have struggled by pure academics to reach where they are.
Ako-Aya, what of these other Bees who are most experienced and qualified but are being sat on?
Please help us and do not hesitate to inform the public.

"'Your good, Interested Reader

"G.R.A. Bota.'

"Dear Sir,

"You surely are an interested reader. Do you belong to the majority Bees or minority bees? If it is with the Four then how did you get there?
"AKO-AYA

v) <u>"FRIDAY APRIL 16, 1971: MBANA E</u>

"Some say I am heartless because of the fact that I did work overtime but I'm not so heart-less as others think. I don't write about a dead, I have the respect for the dead, that is why as a rascally small boy my father was flog-ging me and I ran to the bush and he pursued me and he fell inside a trap and died I still spoke and speak good of him but let the dead bury their dead.

"If somebody in authority employs his tribes men, somebody in either the civil service or statutory corporation he is said to be tribalistic, but do you know the DIYO wanted 'carriers' to carry both him, his wife and his loads into the bush, the Chief got only his village people to do the work. The chief was never accused of tribalism - with this explanation the stage was laid where we passed through Douala to Yaounde. In Douala, I was surprised to find out that the Douala language has replaced the two official languages. At the train station, at the restaurant to speak to a woman it was always 'Mbana E' so these three men from the West maybe 'unwise men from the West' tagged me along and the journey took twelve long hours to the capital, we were bound to the North of Cameroon to shake hands with General Gowon and ask him few questions.

"The morning in Yaounde we found our 'Mbana E' changed to its equivalent of 'Makarana Oh.'

"The three publishers started a tour in Yaounde to see some English people. In Yaounde if you are from West Cameroon, you are English. 'Oh we'll come to see you at the hotel in the evening' most of them told us, but do you know none came. When next some friend from Yaounde comes to West Cameroon, don't bother buying him a drink - Yaounde, he will dodge from you. The perpetual cry is 'brokerage.'

"I fear to describe the amount of beer the publishers drank that first evening or the woman who carried a picture of her husband and children brandishing it at us 'I be married woman with Etat Civile' - she didn't say what a married woman was doing in a hotel at midnight.

"At five, the next morning we emplaned for North. I am not going in this issue to tell you about the north - its beauty, its pictures and its glory, I am going to tell you about this girl 'with a nose like a hawk', a cousin of a VIP to whom getting married to ensure a big post all your life 'as most people dew di do."

"I am going to continue to tell you about this ten percent deal. The offerer, seeing that his money was long delayed and wanting it as all of us do, made the offer of the ten percent. But I visited the building, several cracks, the reinforced frontage cracks, soak - always etc. not complete, yet he was wanting complete pay. Oh he said he was wanting payment for the bit he has completed.

"This ten percent deal are causing a lot of trouble these days, they are even asking for ten percent of your salary and if you are a woman, one day of ten you should be for them alone.
"As I said, I don't know why they hit on figure ten."

vi) <u>"FRIDAY OCT. 15, 1971; SPEAKING FROM MY HEART</u>

"There are certain periods in my life when I like to speak seriously. At such moments I tell the blunt truth and often damn the consequences like this Dahomean name 'Egble makou' speak and die.

"But why shouldn't I speak out, when I had to hide under a seat in the plane all the way to Ethiopia, I returned in time to carry on my thankless work in this big town. I call it thank-less, because if the reverse were true I would have got a bag of medals by now, "So, I left Victoria for this big town college between Moliwe and Mutengene to address the students on life in town.

"But when I entered the assembly hall where male Angels were the audience the programme was reversed and instead, two big business men who were themselves graduates from that school took up the whole time 'Guest Speaking.'

"I don't know why I am always relegated to the back ground. One of the tutors in this College actually thought I was a vendor and opted to buy a copy of the Outlook I was reading. He said he wanted to read what Ako-Aya had written.

"Then I came back to this town where out of every ten people one is a custom officer and heard that this Obang development woman is threatening to tear me up because I told the world the truth, that she fought it out with her friend for a boy friend.
"Came Tuesday yesterday, and another attack levelled at all news medias in the form of threats crashed down from this big delegate in Buea.

"The man wants to read all scripts from our school before sending them for publication, "Instead of ending there he threatened pub-lishers to bear responsibility of unapproved publications.

"I wonder whether this OM. man also wants to become a Censor. I think these big coats affect some people's ideas in Buea - they make them feel bigger and bigger than their bulk or rank really spells for them.

"I wanted to start off with my Ethiopia story at once, about beauties and the rest, but that can wait till my publisher arrives to give the O.K. before I publish. I will rather confine myself with this small football club excos in Victoria.
"Everybody wants to be a club President, yet none of the clubs is likely to show face beyond one year in Division one.

"Remember I am speaking from the bottom of my heart. I feel strongly that a club merger is necessary if Victoria, like the big city of Nkongsamba across the Mungo, will make any head-way in the top Division of Cameroon football.

Chapter Two: Ako-Aya Against Tribalism

"A conspicuous advertisement at the Victoria round about is calling everybody to donate money for the construction of the Centenary Stadium. "I wonder how much has come in yet but the empty drum walls are already crumpling down.

"Can't the highest authorities in this town call these big tycoons for a meeting on this issue? People are battering me right and left, stopping me from publishing this or that. For true, this world don hard."

Chapter Three

Ako-Aya Exposes: The Vices of Certain House-Wives

In the opening article below, 'WHO is MADAM', Ako-Aya attempted to define the status of a housewife. Surprisingly, his subsequent articles on this subject mainly revealed indecent practices perpetrated by married women. In one week, it was the story of a house-wife who had committed abortion because the husband was soon to return from England; or the story of a man going out with his friend's wife. It deteriorated to the stage whereby according to Ako-Aya, even prostitutes could advance criticisms on the flirtatious proclivities of certain married women. He did not forget to narrate the story of the in-fighting that normally goes on in polygamous homes, and openly regretted the fact that house-wives too consulted charlatans. In fact, Ako-Aya shocked his readers when he pointed out that some house-wives merely shed crocodile tears when their husbands die.

"He wrote:

i) <u>"FRIDAY FEB. 26 , 1971: WHO IS MADAM?</u>

l used to think that every woman married to a husband either by native law and customs or Etat Civile) or these other marriages whereby a priest or a Prefect or even a newspaper Editor officiates can rightly be addressed Madam. Thus if I swindled some money tomorrow and got married to this Ibo girl at the bank she could correctly be addressed Madam Ako-Aya.

"By the way a prominent member of the Bank Workers Union in the peoples Bank has asked me fervently to thank chief Arrey for his pungent letter to the editor of this paper. I hardly agree with the views of this paper on this un-Cameroonisation policy but there are many things which we underline must put up with our superiors. Take for example this girl who used to stay in three (3) rooms, this girl who comfortably housed her ageing mother in one of the rooms now moving into one. What of this other one whose mother came down from the village near Oku where I went because the mother saw her picture in the papers.

"So as I was saying we moved to this new place in the municipality. Beach something and there we met a former man's wife - not in the sense of the man but of the woman. In my usual civic or is it servile way I greeted her 'Good Evening, Madam.' Now this former person is now again properly married.

"Then started a strange discussion after we had left Beach. 'That, woman, no madam sef', a girl asked me, she been dey madam time whe - he been married he.' Even when I tried to explain that she was now properly married, my argument fell on deaf ears.

"The truth about it is that us poor men's wives are never addressed madam except Mas. Madam goes to big people's wives. Strange that a woman warned in the papers that she should not be addressed Madam 'dem di spoil my garri', she said.

ii) "FRIDAY MARCH 5, 1971: I DON MUF BELLE

"I do not care much for children even if you think one callous, I feel it is wrong for a human being to spend over half his life looking after 'the young.' Think of it from child birth to University you are still looking after one human being multiply this trouble by the ten children each of us want to raise and the work involved is just gallingi.

"But my woman she thinks differently about them. She would very much want to have children but we just

Chapter Three: Ako-Aya - The Vices of Certain House-Wives

cannot have any. I do not care because if a friend does not pass me 'Ngange' I would not mind so if I cannot be given, what do I care.

"By the way don't think I should have a job before getting children? My father is doing everything possible for we to get this job at my own term. In short I was 5 million francs a year after all my other two brothers earn the same amount in this our father's industry.

"Forty years ago we- were joined in wedlock till a few months ago. She told me she was expecting a baby. The Doctor said she must eat rice, pork, chuku-chuku beaf, no cocoyams but rice, yams and irish potatoes. I bought all these and she started growing fat and I mistook that for the baby.

"One year passed and there was no baby but just when I returned from over she told me 'I don muf Belle' and made some witnesses swear to me that this was true.

"When she 'carried the belle' I had to buy a lot of dresses as well as at her instance send some money to her parents. I even opened a bank account for the baby in her name. I have however realised that this 'na so-so lie-lie.'

"Because of this and other matters I am determined to marry a second wife and you can read about the second wife Monica now sweeping the whole country in the next issue.

iii)   "WEDNESDAY APRIL, 14. 1971: I DI WORK OVERTIME

"I used to hear it said that a man should either die because of money or because of woman. Little did I dream that this could happen in my life time. I have learnt to believe that death comes only at old age when all tiny molecules that this body is made wither and die.

"As I say I have doubted the sincerity of church goers. So when during Easter I saw processions and he had not come to make his peace with me, I just wondered.

"So my wife telephoned me the other day she was not coming home after work as she was scheduled to do overtime. After that she was going to attend a meeting in the church - one of these fellowship things.

"As usual when one grows old and is married to a young girl, one tends to love her more and so I am or was deeply attached to my former, wife Former, not in the sense that we divorced, but in the sense that she would be a cripple all her life and so is not a wife.

"Overtime and church meeting turned to eating of roasted fish at the Mungo Brigade, where my wife was heading to. You know I had warned this man to please leave my wife alone but you can't stop a cat from musing and my warning fell on deaf ears. You remember I wrote sometimes about my tour of a plantation and this big man taking this small man's wife and he quoted the Book 'He that has to him more shall be given but he that has not even that which he has shall be taken away - very few understood me then.

"How many of us pre tend that we are working overtime and yet we are merely creating rendez-vous for our girl/boyfriends. You hear them say 'I am going back to the office' and near the office a girl is already waiting.

"These journalists paid for me to go to Garoua with them - in the next issue I will tell you all about the trip - the Northern beautiful girls, Western civilization, not to forget the continuation of the ten percent deal. These and many more are yours during the next issue.

Chapter Three: Ako-Aya - The Vices of Certain House-Wives

iii)   "FRIDAY APRIL 23, 1971; MY FRIEND'S WIFE

"I sometimes shudder at these marriage vows, they are so binding I would never think of breaking.

"... to have and to hold for better or for worse, for richer or for poorer, until death do us part.' I think death do us part should be substituted in our present age to 'poverty' do us part.

"How else can I say it when I see the way some wives treat their husbands who for no fault of theirs have lost their employment. Some of them now sneer at such husbands - 'You no de go drink again' she would ask?

"So I visited such a friend and his wife last weekend. Believe me I wept when we came back at night without food, not because I was hungry but because the answer to our question was 'una no get hand for cook.' Mark you it was midnight and she had only just come home. 'I be go drink with my friend dem.' Well friend is common gender and we were not to know whether the friends were males or females.

"We slept without food and in the morning she slept on and on not caring to wake up and prepare breakfast for us. She left for work, taking the keys of the cupboard which contained breakfast things. 'Buy una own' she shouted back when we asked for the key.

"This was a wife who was 'jelosing' her husband when he was working and earning a good salary. "This is a woman who fought other women because of her husband, now however the scales are turned, and life is like that."

iv) "WEDNESDAY SEPT. 1, 1971:
SOME MAN DEY UNDER BED

"Since my mother gave birth to me and I became her twelfth son I have always maintained that the whole world lives on credit, and even then I always recognised both my parents as agents of my creation.

"But today the world is different. How else can I say, when children as young as four years of age cannot recognise their own parents. "Even though everybody is blaming me for letting myself be overtaken by events, I will not write about this new collapsing fit nor about this quartite send-off, retirement and reception party at the rocks club yesterday.

"I want to look into these cases that set flying to pieces last weekend in Victoria. "It has never occurred to me that children of four can remember the man they see 'Biting their Mami's mouth' every night when they see him again in broad day-light.

"And so Mr. X of this Cassava Farm at Victoria never suspected his wife of anything silly during his two weeks routine tour to Kumba, until he carried his four year old son and went strolling along Church Street one evening.

"The child imitated him when he pointed to a tall young man dressed in eye attire and cried 'see my papa eh left me, ah go for my papa."

"Mr. X couldn't understand this at all, that his own son should recognise another man and call him "my papa» meanwhile the young man turned his face and walked to a different direction.

"The man had a job or work to do explaining, yes, and parking out.

"But that is the way things are and unless decree N°251 is enforced right down to the children how can that order of children change?

"This other child at Gardens sleeps with her parents and so it didn't surprise her when her mother told her at midnight one day that her father was back from his trip. After all the man who undressed and slept in front was just as tall as daddy and the child was merely three years old.

"But when shortly afterwards another man banged on the door and came into the house, the child woke up, confused. The man on the bed went under the bed.
"Mr. Joach... didn't notice anything wrong in his room as he undressed saw that his daughter was still awake and kept looking under the bed.

"'Hello Commy come up and sleep' he called, but the child did not move. 'Papa, ah di fear da man under bed'. The mother tried to close the child's mouth with a bedsheet, but the deal was out and Mr. Joach jumped out of the bed to see for himself.

"It was the tortoise who said, there is nothing wrong with tricks if only you know how to play them.

"The lights went out and when the man under-bed rushed out of the room, God alone knows.

"That was another marriage gone to hell."

vi) <u>"THURSDAY SEPT. 9, 1971: I BE WORKING CLASS</u>

My brother, one of these early University graduates was going to get married to a pupil teacher in our village. It was those days when very few girls went to school and those who worked were looked on as some thing from space. Then the girl's father was demanding two hundred pounds because my pikin be working class.'

"Today there are so many of the 'working class' that they don't appear any more important.

"'My girl-friend na working class' used to be the boast of a few years back but today you are important if your girl-friend is 'shome' or especiale so with all the new regulations about working women, I am surprised that these working class are still 'Trowering babies. This time house wives have joined in this dangerous game in a country which is sparsely populated. "But talking about these working class or recent girls who work in pubs are also calling them-selves working class. Their salaries are by negotiation and do not come up to 2.000 francs a month. They are being exploited as usual and even 'gregory' does not appear to help them yet how many of us shout 'savis' everyday in the pubs.

"I sat in one of these, hearing them discuss on what I wrote yesterday the tall one was fuming and saying, that if he lost his job he would take a matchet after me. Another said that he wondered why I was not locked up. Better to say this than shut up and allow greed eat deep into the fabric of our society.

"I suggest that next time a baby is found in a pit latrine or in the bush the mother should be tried and made for a firing squad."

vii) <u>FRIDAY NOV. 12, 1971:
YAWINDE SISTER</u>

"When my column was given a blackout the other day I received a warning from my publisher reminding me that he may reverse the pages of my file back to the date of the termination letter he served me early this year. He still feels very concerned about the loss I caused on that establishment. And to help him keep this off his mind, he has threatened to force me home on leave. I enjoy seeing my articles on papers and pen and paper have become part of my life. But one thing I feed at home is this long chain of relatives.

"Always you hear your grand mother introducing you to a beautiful girl as your father's grand mother's sister's daughter until you get confused about these your sisters, whether to accept them as such or not. Therefore to some, this numbering of cousins from first to the twentieth is what is intriguing even to diplomats what they called Yawinde sister. Take this one diplomat who just returned from home on leave, A chain of sisters were introduced to him even though he remembers only himself, a brother and a sister as the only births of his mother's womb.

"He feels head-long on one of them only to board the plane over night. The affair is producing flames within family circles.

"So when some body tells you 'Voila ma soeur.' This is my sister, do not believe. They can well be husband and wife or boy and girl-friend.

"But didn't I say I would bring you the other side of 'Kaiful for Victoria friend.' well the scene is again around this motor Company that sells second-hand cars and an Indian child was born in this typically Cameroonian family. Divorce followed but who knows whether some of us Cameroonians have Indian blood in us.

So of course she hob nobbed with the swindler and got another baby and this tall young man fell prey to her. This did not exclude her setting other men from Muyuka to Bamenda and the one she calls her friend at all but a woman she had all the time cheated. They say the Devil laughs when a thief steals from another and the Devil does the same when a friend cheats a friend. So having cheated a friend, the friend has now got her own back and has virtually become whore.»

viii) "TUESDAY NOV. 16, 1971: WEEKEND RETURNS AH DON GET MISSION MEDAL

"I was talking to some Cameroonian beauties over the weekend and the subject changed to marriage. It appears youngmen have very little chances these days marriage-wise. They said they should prefer men of 40 and over preferably somebody who had divorced his first wife with one or two children and no sister or mother living.

"Well perennial lack of husband is a problem which must be looked into by our Economists. But while some 'cry' husbands others do not care about their husband. Take this big CDC woman who stealthily went to visit her boy friend's sick father or this Balundu married nurse whose husband had to pull strings in order for her to do a nursing aid's course - there is no difference between her house and the fence in Kumba.

"So I went to Tiko again during the weekend; set aside all the engagements I had in Buea. Some kind people were to keep 'Kpakoko' for me but even this did not tempt me despite the fact that I went there.

"I went to this Catholic Bazaar and just as I got to the gate one of these white women dressed in white from head to toe blocked my way. In a flash she pinned a decoration on my chest saying as she did so, 'Government medals maybe finished Mr. Ako-Aya and so you can't be decorated, but we of the mission also see your good work. I endow you with the 1st class medal Order of Merit.'

Chapter Three: Ako-Aya - The Vices of Certain House-Wives

"Then I begged a ride in one of these cars where the driver connects two wires to ignite the engine and stopped over at this aviasion hotel to see what the Tiko Tea time dance looks like.

"Whether that was good luck or not God alone knows but my legs carried me straight to a seat where this stores-girl-turned mistress was sitting with a bevy of subordinates.

"She brought them including this puf-puf girl, then he had to take permission from their queen Elizabeth II.

"The queen herself was an ex-student of this big college in the Cross River Town but she got pregnant in form two and went into hiding in idle.

"I had no trouble with the girl personally, in fact, I almost fell for her, but when she became proud and spoke to people anyhow I recoiled like a snake feeling that ugly as I am, I have better manners.

"You remember this ship that came from Bamenda with tons of garri to Tiko and sold very cheaply. The people who own Tiko market bought this garri and after selling some of it reported to the health people and it was condemned. By this trick the Bamenda people went up and the garri was not paid for.

"This same garri was bought by other food contractors and it was not condemned. Something has to be done in this Tiko about these Ibo Taxis that 'catch' others for running during the curfew. The injustices are becoming very apparent and where barbers become butchers or Doctors and Magistrates go down to do the work of Police men, the justice should not only be done but seen to be done.

"I shuffled to Victoria where business has become so bad that even some women by preparing for Xmas have started stealing from traders. We went to the Bell to chop river and it was full. Vocalist Ngassa was at his best. Millie and Lucy did not come - two of my new found friends and I decided to call it a day. But the usual clientelle was there tankers and the rest."

ix)   "TUESDAY OCT. 23, 2973: I GO DIE TODAY"

"'I go die today', 'I go die today', a woman whose husband died was crying. At the grave-yard she fell inside the grave desiring to be buried with the man she loved.
"But my dear reader before a week was out, I found her in long black flowing robes dancing to the tunes of Ekambi Brilliant. You should have really knocked me down with a feather.

"As soon as she saw me she started raining abuses on me, 'Go write' she shouted. I hear she smokes 'banga' and is a drug addict. Do I blame her.

"Well today I promised writing about this new house-boy I have just taken on. We will call his name John.

"John when you go market today buy only short okro not the long ones.

"John when you cook soup for me, taste only the salt not the pepper.

"John when I send you to my gfs do not tell them I am building a house.

"John, well I gave John so many instructions and rules and regulations that John told me 'Massa I no go work, your Iowa dew too plenty. No man fit keep them.'

Chapter Three: Ako-Aya - The Vices of Certain House-Wives

"Well, if John cannot keep such laws who will keep them. I must look for another house-boy.

"Man, you must also go to the Capital as often as I go. In some parts of the city elegant buildings all taken over by people. Yet our favoured class of people do not want to stay there because of this 20% rent allowance.

"I must praise the big men of this ghost town. They are giving people houses by force so this 20% can be used for other development."

x) **"WEDNESDAY JULY 21, 1976: NA MBANYA VERSUS MBANYA NOW**

"A weekend visit carried me to several parts of the country. In each town na so so trouble for marret woman.

"These days most house wives dress with little difference from free girls. In one of these road junction towns, there was a heavy scuffle between massa and woman because the house wife refused to subject herself to her. senior mates.

"That's why it is not good for marret plenty woman them even though it is not an offence.

"In Kumba, there was another serious disagreement between a boy and girl friend. She was beaten mercilessly and almost stripped to the waist.

"Lido pop i dong ton na place for disappointment for lovers. They say she be na student for the big school in Kumba. Yes like harlot like student.

xi) **"FRIDAY NOV. 12, 1976:
EVEN HOUSE-WIVES TOO DEM DONG
ENTER MUNGANG NOW**

"With the continued explosion of the woman population, marret di hard now. Because of hard-ship boys don't like to marry these days. And so this my friend's wife decided to go the mungang way in order to end the affair between her man and this Council lady.

"She struggled in vain for long to deter her man from seeing VRC husband grabber and decided only pins could do the job, so she used them. 'My brother lef me. Dis tarn wey man pickin dem no want marret again. If man play with yi husband na yi sef go cry after.' I met her talking to a friend.

"I get angry when I hear how much money the advanced countries spend on going to the moon alone. Why can't they try and manufacture a drug that can make a man stop drinking. Massa, until palmy go finish man no go hear fine. No bi mumbi dis - Go to street 6 in Tiko and unless you know how to use your words you would buy afofo for kerosene.

"'Na hot or cold kerosene you want', one lady passing as a kerosene seller along the road asked me and until I found out later then did I know that cold kerosene is real one and hot kerosene means afofo.

"Here in Victoria Hospital staff have begun a new deal. Very soon one won't be operated because of lack of spirit. No spirit hah de reign now for town.

"Back to town, can I talk about this architect, metuseller beauty, who was nearly beaten by mbanya nyi pikin dem, because Miss Architect de vex say Miss Banker de take nyi jumba."

Chapter Four

Ako-Aya and Prostitution

Ako-Aya unilaterally appointed himself leader of all the prostitutes in former West Cameroon. Indeed, in his article 'NKANNE DONG BURN', he spelt out the main prostitution centres, namely, Nkanne in Douala, Church Street in Victoria, Ibo Quarters at Fiango in Kumba, and Abakwa in Bamenda. Throughout his writi5ngs, one notices phrases such as 'my army', hiy team', all of which referred to prosti-tutes. It is difficult to say whether or not Ako-Aya har-boured a dirty mind; or was it that as a mature writer, he was condemned to use words in their right places even if their connotations affected our own sense of decency?

All in all, Ako-Aya condemned prostitution, especially as it often generated open quarrels over tycoons. Indeed, he laughed at them during periods of economic decline as his article 'The World Don Hard' would show.

He wrote:

i) "TUESDAY FEB. 23, 1971 TWO AT A BLOW

"One thing I like of us Cameroonians is that we always kill two birds with one stone or as we say in school language - Two at a blow. Take this VIP (Very Inferior Person) who is not only satis-fied with his post but owns a housing estate. What of this other one with a big transport service on top of everything else, and yet I am not sure of the next meal.

"As if this 'two at a blow' attitude should only be for men, lately the girls have got it into them. Thus first one boy friend is not sufficient but two, one of them must be a married man. And so it was that last weekend a girl resident in one of our many places who go by the name hotels had an offer of a free bed and loding for a night. She started by asking for 5000 francs, there was haggling till at last it was 2.300 frs or so many German Marks. During the prelimina-ries, that is shots of whisky another stranger made the same offer and again another 2.300 frs. The two men stay in the same room in the hotel and this girl had all the two beds to herself. Next morning the hospital provided her with another bed and she had to get blood transfusion as she had lost so much blood. What of the 4.600 frs you ask well it was found in her purse. "Take - Ma for instance with her profession. This is not sufficient but she must double in house building. The house completed and she applies for electricity. An estimate is worked for 52 thousand francs, but you see if I was the girl, I would have been wade to pay that amount but with her they asked her to pay only fifteen thousand francs an official who also gets two at a blow, his salary and the means of retaining - Ma.

"I received a very interesting letter from a reader in Tiko and here it is:-

"'Dr. AKO-AYA ON SAFETY FIRST RULE"

"'Dear Editor,

"'In fact, I bought my Outlook from a Passer-by vendor, I went over the issue at the last page '4' I noticed Ako-Aya as an educator, a traveller who can see, and also an intelligent writer. I am therefore saying that AKO-AYA deserves praise. He, the patient from Oku is telling you, about apolo disease of the eyes, then another sudden disease 'krola' which can kill immediately. Another one may come again after krola and that may be 'Beriberi' disease. Doctor Ako-Aya graduated on Safe First-Rule from Oku. He wrote krola injection, or innoculation may help little, but keep to your safety first Rule for the pre-ventives of any further disease. I thank you Dr. AKO-AYA for your advice."

Chapter Four: Ako-Aya and Prostitution

ii) "FRIDAY MAY, 28, 1971:
I GET MONEY, I GO MARKET YOU"

"Our people say an antelope killed in a hunting expedition never blames the killer but the man who organised the trip. And because all lizards move on their bellies, one can not tell which of the lizards has belle ache. And so after last week's kale kale we have our antelopes in our midst.

"When, even road masters like this big 'Vee I owe' were temporarily stripped of their powers from God. I remember one more saying that a tortoise never catches head ache until its shell has been removed. That's how I saw it and like that lizard with belly ache among other lizards moving on their bellies, two friends down the coast were having their share of belly ache. Both friends working in different government depart-merits are asking a hand of love of a certain girl also down the coast - both suitors have presented themselves to the father of the girl but them man like his daughter is not decided yet on who to accept. I hear things have changed and that parents no longer select husbands for their daughters, not even wives for their sons. Normally the campaign continued underground between the two suitors with verging tactics. One of them laid hands on the pay-slips to the parents of the girl to compare who earns higher and who is capable of making his daughter happy as a husband.

"The girl I understand has lost her head for the low paid boy but the father has been enticed by the fat pay slip. So a family adviser an old woman told the girl 's father that he should not think like the baby monkey who, after having eaten told its mother to pull off the teeth, forgetting that it will feel hungry again.

"The girl too I hear was going round the town looking for him and what with the crowds rushing pell mell to see our head of state, they lost each other in the confusion poor devil. I hear the boy with low pay had threatened to seek legal redress from the other friend but legal redress or no legal redress that's not my business now.

"What about this big journalist whose name is bigger than his person, who went about the whole town of Victoria two days ago in big jumper with worn-out shoes in search of a girl-friend who was supposed to have come from Kumba?

"Left to me, whenever the President is visiting us all girls should be called up and guarded in jungle village - that is the safest way to get everybody in there."

ii) "TUESDAY JUNE, 15 1971: CHANGING COLOURS

"Was it not James Brown who sang 'Say loud, I am black and proud' and was it not Aggray of Africa who taught us that just as a piano has white and black keys to produce good music, the creator made human beings white and black for the good of the human race.

"But this black colour given us or is it coffee brown in spited by most of us and Europeans are forming this hatred for our colour for their own purposes.

"How else can I explain this when many dark Cameroon beauties have suddenly become 'white.' There are bleaching products. Kumba and the East are added but in Kumba last week, this local manufacture burnt a girl's face.

"Take this other woman who is in fact a leper, she used the local bleaching and hurt the leprosy marks and all so that her face is now as light as the area occupied by leprosy but the deadly disease has pately developed an even white colour.

"One would think this sort of thing would be done by only the teenage, but grannies and grand-dads have also joined the band wagon.

"Another sister lost her husband and the money to buy the ointments was not there and she turned back - just like a chameleon does.

"Let us be proud of our colour and not imitate foolish things."

iv) "TUESDAY AUGUST 24, 1971: AH PI GO FOR POLICE

"When people started attacking me for being ungrateful I begin to wonder whether I shouldn't give up in 'education' the public.

"How can I be termed ungrateful when people like beautiful Miss Julsick who is attached to those big delegates of culture in Buea decided to double cross his prominent Cameroonian who is contemplating on abandoning his profession for business.

"There are times when people let their anger to overcome their reason and nobody can give judge-ment on the out-come of such short out-bursts. "But the one which took place recently at Buea wasn't just a display of anger, it was a real show down.

"Two Mercedez-Benz cars were parked outside her house when the Policeman who had furnished it from Gas Cooker, Dumlopillo to the very carpet on the floor was busy inside. I couldn't help suppressing a smile when I understood that this girl had kept out of sight of the business man for almost a week, simply because a 'doctor' without a hospital from overseas was around town. "In less than twenty minutes the job was done and out came the large Vono family bed which disappeared into smoke carried away by the businessman, chairs, cooker and cushions and all the rest.

"A one-time semi-paradise was in twenty minutes transformed into a dancing hall a typical reward for ungratefulness, and as the cars drove off, lovely Miss Julsick who had no where even to sit sat down on a pillar and stared in disbelief.

"The world is a wonderful place and can everybody still say I am ungrateful now?

"What about this woman in Gardens Victoria who decided to abandon her own house because five hefty men 'signed-die' at her door each wanting to take a turn T.D.B.

"She left her door open and told them I di go for call police and disappeared into the night.

"She never came back. Can you guess where she passed the night?

"Wait for the answer next issue."

v) "WEDNESDAY SEPT 15, 1971; AH DI GO FOR BELL HOTEL FOR GO CHOP RIVER

"When the world was younger parents used to push their children to schools and often subjected them to a lot of corporal punishment because they felt that was a sure way to make young ones learn.

Chapter Four: Ako-Aya and Prostitution

"But what can we say about this new age when laws upon laws prohibit the use of the lash and leaders fear even to touch a child with a whip. I have heard of parents who have been jailed because they inflicted corporal punishment on their own children.

"The result of this new fashion is catastrophic, as it has partly contributed to the lowered standards of Education.

"A child in one of the schools I happened to visit yesterday boldly told her teacher 'Why you di nack me, you think say ah biyyour woman?'

"Even when these children leave school some half way through they know only one thing, to rent houses and start life in full swing.

"So it was not surprising when one evening I met one of these beauties from Church Street who has become rather prominent in society recently, dressed like a 'lady' and when I asked where she was going she shouted 'Ah di go for bell hotel to go chop river.'

"It took me over fifteen minutes to decipher this code she had spat out, to understand that she meant to say, she was going to Bay Hotel to eat river.

"Everyday I see men and women of all ages going to attend adult literacy classes, and quite often, I hear of graduation ceremonies, so it beats me when I still meet young, beautiful girls who loiter around our highest men in society, and tourists and I feel really bad when I realize that the adult classes are being ignored by many people who need them. Whether literate or not I don't think a man can forget his own son or a husband his wife.

"But what about this big Labour man with a 404 who denied his own son at Kumba simply because he now has a woman from Yawinde.

"I would have congratulated this man if he had just taken the Yawinde 'come-down' for a second wife, instead of abandoning the Kumba woman with one child alive and the other dead.

"Our understanding Head of State allows wives and what with these family allowances Mr. Ma ... Would be a rich man in Jess than one year.

"He could soon compete favourably with this millionaire in Kumba last week who added to his wealth by taking on a third wife, this time an Ibo.

"If a man can prove that international marriages like this millionaire's can work very well even for a third wife, why can't this Labour man who knows the whole Labour Code off by heart take on his own country girl with whom he has two children?

"I really think I ought to add something to edict 251 and it is this: (1) That anybody caught beating his or her child will be punished also by the whip. (2) Also anybody who abandons his first woman for another shall be punished by a forfeiture of his house which will be given to the ousted woman. This new Edict shall be 251(1)b.
"See you next issue."

iii) "WEDNESDAY OCT. 13, 1971: THE WORLD DON HARD

"One thing keeps me consoled always and that is the fact that all men were born equal. The truism has passed through generations until even in the very composition of my village there are those who count themselves as

Chapter Four: Ako-Aya and Prostitution

the Onasises by their standard Therefore even though I cannot count myself as an Onasis, I have an 'Epse' always to wet my throat down which to me is great. One thing, besides these gun threats in Douala air-port which have kept me sick I look at my world as a happy one, because they say 'poor man coming up in public with such idioms like, 'arata no get plaba with bottro'and so on.

"All the same, without thinking of where to get a husband like this one girl a problem grazing the sky, who works with these Banque Generale de Victoria who keeps paying visits to mile four with a white hen to consult the gods for the possibility of coming across an Onasis as a husband.

"And these drinking schools have had new students most of them bank workers of the female sex who are having an eye on a long I.D. 19 car which is the ideal car. I hear this girl is now finding a world that is hard because an amulet which was given to her intended to help catch a husband who is ready to pay the bill for an I.D. 19.

"What of these 'Obang' girl who fought over the weekend because of a man. And when some of our sisters from mile one take leave of this hard life in Victoria and behind that they are now married in Douala. Only to reappear in the streets again in guerrilla form.

"And while I was meeting the biggest test at the Douala airport our mile one sister scratched a boy's face like a cat. They say it is love. But 'I Ako-Aya, born on the last day of the month in the land of the proud people, this day declare that I shall never fall in love with two girls.' Love has become a battle. I Thomas Ako-Aya, knowing fully well that the world is an unkind place, hereby decree that no man born of a woman should allow his soul to be tortured by the emptiness of this world. This decree shall prohibit any woman playing carelessly with a man's private like the case at Church Street where a woman go t grip of a man's private part because he refused to settle bills.

"I am reluctant to express my fears that these medals, decorations have also gone through the last ten years and I fear that they have run out of stock meaning that I have lost all the chances of getting one since ten anniversary too has left me in the cold.

"The process started ten years ago, beginning from freedom fighters to farmers and even those who foiled attempts by thieves to steal government money.

"It is now I am beginning to feel the pangs of being ignored even though I dive into depths to bring out the most secretary secrets. I am happy that the C.N.U. will live for ever so that we may continue to see justice and peace. "The world don hard."

vii) "TUESDAY OCT. 19, 1971: LETTER FROM MY PUBLISHER"

"I received a letter from my Publisher who was in Ethiopia and have taken the liberty to publish it bellow.

"'Dear Ako,

"'I am sorry about what happened to you at the Douala Airport. One thing wrong with you is that you are a firm believer in 'all men are born equal and they are endowed by their creator with inherent and inallienable rights.'

"Well, all of us are born unequal, there are
those born great, there are those who achieve it enthrusted upon them and there are the rest like you and the best thing to do is for those of us great to look down on you.

Chapter Four: Ako-Aya and Prostitution

"So my dear Aya do not always compare yourself with me too much. I will not write about the serious side of my visit, the news I like to break to you is that I have given up celibacy and have got married, yes to a beautiful Ethiopian wife.

"There is no Ethiopian girl who is not very beautiful - light skin with a healthy crop of curly hair. Here there is no need for the Afro-wig or of Nku cream. The thin air gives them long noses, as long as that of a hawk.

"When you sometimes write about your Church Street episodes, I take it as if you have not sufficiently travelled. There is no Prostitution in Cameroon by the standards here. "A house with red light and a girl standing at the door way beckoning you to come, and there are millions of such houses, is a regular affair. But here the economic theory of the supply affecting demand is exploded because so many prostitutes fee goes up and up and before we left it had hit 20 Ethiopian dollars, the equivalent of 2.000 francs CFA.

"The Ethiopians themselves do not like their women but go in for the whites who come in as tourists, quite a brisk trade goes on between visitors, small boys and women. With the O.A.U., the I.L.O. Africa Regional Headquarters and other International bodies almost everybody from the rest of Africa goes to Addiss. With a dark face the question is always 'Are you here for a Conference?' 'would you like an Ethiopian girl?' If your pride makes you answer 'Conference' then the fees go up by geometric progression.

"Well Ako, I am now properly married just the beginning of promoting African Unity and our first child will be called Haile Selassie.

"The only thing is I will not come with her. I must 'find' money to pay for her ticket. Maybe you, Mbella or Commando will be able to help.

"PUBLISHER."

iv)   "FRIDAY NOV. 5, 1971: GREGORY I GOOD?

"My friend's insurance had expired and he went to renew it. 'Beau' he said, 'I cannot buy you an 'espe' any longer, you must go down to 'Ngangi.' He said the insurance people had increased by about 30% and to service his car, his mechanics had increased about 20%.

"So representation came from Mammy Yao in Fence in Kumba and from Church Street in Victoria, observers came from Buea and Tiko. The aim of this conference was to increase cost of landing charges. I didn't know by how many percent this has gone up but I hear after pay 500 francs is the least amount at any time whilst 'when moon don go' the cost will remain the same as previously and that is at 250 francs.

"So I say this Gregory thing is good and bad -good that we are all having a lot of money now even though our friends are being removed from work for 'reorganisation' but bad that we are paying more for the things we have been used to getting cheaper.

"Because of Gregory and its effects, I aw constrained to make an amendment to edict 251, Art, 1. The whole of the hours of any body's life time in Cameroon have been declared drinking hours.

"Art, 2. Only essential workers need work and by this is meant farmers and fisher men only. "Art, 3. Any body in Cameroon caught drinking during working hours, that is his life-time will be made to drink 101/2 times more each day. "Art. 4. All Brewers are asked to step up pro-duction and they are to enforce this order assisted by the force as before mentioned."

v) "WEDNESDAY DEC. 1, 1971:
YOU BELLE DON SPOIL

"That's always the case when girls begin to leave their fellow men's folk here in Africa and go all out for the white man from Europe. "It is not that her 'belle' really got spoilt. It was not even because she went after a white man for that matter, her friends were just jealous of her because she was befriending a white one of these lankyt Ashen faced boys from over the seas who spent all their nights in this Mira... Hotel near the sea.

"The girl herself was one of this dotted beauties who looked least a beauty, they scratched it out with this other queen Mary at this Kam spot in Gardens Victoria who has thighs as thick as a jug.

"Their quarrel had no meaning, but they disturbed the whole of Gardens until two O'clock in the night. Before I could get the sense of what they were shouting at each other, one of them shouted at the other 'You belle don spol' and the other cut of 'you dry like Mbonga."

"I know I am not strong to divide fights but I hate to see girls fighting especially for men let alone a 'Whiteman'.
"I went to this capital town and peeped into one of these tribunals only to stop dead when I saw three judges busy on a case. I hate to be charged for contempt, so I sat down quietly to hear what the case was all about and what did I hear but another case of girls fighting.

"I strained my flappy ears and only caught words like Julsik, Helbaga and 'fought after one threw the other's good' or so I heard. I have a very bad memory these

days, but I shuffled along to this farm made of lower houses hence the name lower farms and tried to pay a visit. There is a girl in Buea Prisons in captivity. This girl has never been found guilty and sentenced, in fact she is innocent. A girl of that age with murderers and hardened criminals her colleagues, a maybe future wife of a maybe President. Yet none of us does anything to rescue her.
"Because her mother Esther is serving a jail sentence and has no relatives who can take care of her. The mother was a former Central Bank Worker.

"What to do, allow this three yearling continue in captivity or release the mother (at least for the girl's sake and suspend the remainder sentence). Have you a three yearling, then think of one who will spend Xmas in jail what to do.
"So with these thoughts weighing heavily in my mind I ..."

Chapter Five

Ako-Aya and Women from the East

When the Tiko-Douala highway was constructed, there was immediately witnessed an influx of prostitutes from Douala to Victoria. And as Ako-Aya rightly pointed out, the competition between these people stepped up drastically. He equally alluded to the arguments raised by others that there were many incidental benefits which would flow when one got married to any of these girls from the 'East', viz, money, promotion and security at job-site.

He wrote:

i) <u>"WEDNESDAY FEB. 24, 1971;
NA WAR-0</u>

"My mother loved her husband to the very end and to her my father was her life, her income, her all. This is why she calls my father 'papa.' "But times have changed from then till now and nobody knows what a woman wants. How can any man know, when just yesterday this beauty was riding in Mercedez cars in Buea and today she runs after footballers in the pops. She can no longer buy creams, to lighten her skin and she is turning to' dark in patches like a hideous cameleon. 'No mind all that big motor dem' she confided in me, 'na so so debt.' She continued, 'VIP mean very indebted person.'

"Take this daughter of a Reverend who almost murdered our very clever big man. She used to stay in a big house with servants and cars and her physical and mental cruelty to the man she swore to have and to hold for richer for poorer until riches do us part.

"To some people like myself poverty makes us part but to the capital clique it is riches that do them part.

First it was this educationist, then this labourer now it is this P. & T. worker -all divorcing their wives and taking on beauties from East.

"Some say if you marry from the East you are sure of lasting appointment and others say marry from the East and you become very rich. So the man from Yaounde came to get married to my sister and I said 'No' because you will very soon leave her and marry a long neck from the East."

ii)   "TUESDAY MARCH 2, 1971; NA MAN DI LOSS"

'I used to wonder why my mother kept telling me how she suffered for me and how she felt pains when she brought me to life and I always asked her why didn't you come out myself. She always ended with the expression 'NA WOMAN DI LOSS'. "But how can that be when just the other day a rich gentleman, one of these men who earn lots of money for keeping peace brought in a beauty from 'Douala' for the week-end.

"He thought that he was just going to have a good time. You know, lots of kisses, beck, Meta Heineken and maybe some temporary accommodation in some of these posh hotels. In short he wanted to spend not more than five thousand francs for the weekend. When this beauty arrives in the man's house, she sniffed around the place like a dog that has scented a strange smell.

"The man asked her to sit down at table, but she shook her head. 'I no di "manger" for cholera plate.' 'That was something like an insult that his plates were dirty, but the man didn't mind it.

"He carried her to this expensive hotel at the beach and she ate a whole chicken and drank five shots of cinzano all amounting to 4.500 francs.

Chapter Five: Ako-Aya and Women from the East

"Back home, lets call the man Mr. Wanted Her, but the beauty laughed and whispered into the man's ear. 'I been seen rat under pillow.' This man could not believe his ears. He called in his junior brother and gave him a sound beating for keeping his bed dirty. Then they left for the hotel again.

"This time his temporary accommodation receipt reads 3.500 frs. for two and a half hours.

"The fun in the whole thing is that they slept on that bed when they got back home without anymore talk of rats. When Mr. G. asked me, she turned her back on him murmuring, 'I been see my time for hotel' and that was all.

"The next morning this beauty asked the man to take her to Pritannia. There again 5.000 frs went for a 'pardessus.' She refused to travel by public transport 'detn too dorty' and left by hired car. For 5.000 frs Mr. G. sat down to add up the amount he had spent and realised that he has spent 18.000 francs.

"When his friend called at his house and heard his story Mr. G. shrugged his broad shoulder 'Na Man di Loss' he told his friend.

"The craze this day is on Afro-wigs and foolish me, I met this cousin who will very soon be consigning me to jail and I thought it was her natural hair. But can you describe the horror when I saw her true hair being plaited by a mother - no swindler doled out 5 thou here though.

"But the Afro-craze has caught on and some are in for the biggest wigs that weigh on them like lead.

"Look at the bead this court girl or of this Nyanga Obang girl I pity them for loads they carry. First it was English wigs, now Afro-wigs and soon maybe Cameroon wigs - well, why can't they be natural.

"There are a lot of false things one goes in for these days - hair burst, buttocks and all, and all these in the name of civilization.
"More till next issue."

iii) Hi) "TUESDAY SEPT. 22, 1971: WHAT A WEEK-END(2)

"Hundreds of readers have written to ask that our Tuesday paper should regularly bear the exploits of the week-end and who am I, not to accede to readers' request. Among several of those who wrote, were letters from house-wives believing that I will write about the goings-on of their husbands. Here I think they will be disappointed for rather than breaking homes, I will rather see more marriages contracted.

"'Ako-Aya', my publisher told me, get ready for us to go to Douala, this Ethiopian Airlines people have thrown another invitation. And so Friday found me at a plosh hotel in Douala, wine women everything. I dread to write about what these three 'English' men did, I even dread to repeat the word 'Half Measures' for in this municipality, a beautiful girl moves from hotel to hotel for a quick one till around midnight she settles into one of them. The intake is around ten thousand. But I like these Douala beauties. You merely sit with the reception -slim or pumpy full or half burst and provided you are anxious to spend money, the goods are delivered to you. Contrast these with our West Cameroon beauties, with their lack of husbands where you must bribe your way with 'Especiale' and Beck and Soya before the green lights are shown you, and the setting must be at the Atlantic Beach and you must go home around three. "So I moved from Douala to Tiko where the road I complained of has had its own quota of sea-wall , no more any muf -belle, thanks to all. I reached Victoria and 'Winter Brothers' brought in a truck load of Bamenda beauties and they were intent on taking the town by storm. Tall and hefty, middle size and middle-age beautiful without make-up they were intent on what they wanted - money. The same strategy as the Douala ones 'make we go for your house now then I come back.' Few of us don' t want half measures but they all ended at the Atlantic Beach.

"Everybody who is any one was there inclusive of 3 Nkambe people their white wives, Douala and Victoria should send up some girls to Nkambe. Three Nkambe's have three white wives and none of this people ever marry from their tribes. Either they have no woman up there or they don't send them to school or - well I leave you to guess.

"Our tables were all black and 'we lef plenty mimbo.' I have suggested that there should be no work on Monday because of this Mimbo palaver.
"'Massa nobi Mimbo dis.'"

iv) "TUESDAY OCT. 26, 1971: GIVE ME WAN BEER SPECIAL WEEK-END REPORT

"The week-end began with a band, not because I had a knock on my head but because the banks were full on Friday with civil servants. Up in Buea it was a real struggle. 'How I go manage go Victoria if I no take pay', many of them appealed to the counter clerks. Well on Fridays the Banks close their doors only at 2 p.m. and everybody went home happy.

"In Buea you can almost join a taxi free from the town to the clerks quarters. All you need is a coat and tie, and at the quarters ask the driver if he can change 1.000 Francs of course even if he can, he is not going to do it for 10 francs and you can walk away cooly. Anyway I came down with several of them, the heat in Victoria was no sufficient reason for them to remove their oats.

"As everybody was coming to the coast, I did not find it necessary to leave the town. There were all sorts of people and one wonders if they had like in Addis (so my publisher says) come to attend 'meetings' these days but conference.'

"The Victoria beauties recognise money when they see it and if they saw a 'coated' man it would be 'Give me wan bear'. Of course when the pocket is full, kindness comes easily and so the Standard and City were all full. But the Bay was a bigger attraction and we all went there.
"Our sisters from Douala, know Government 'pay time' and there were so many, you would think it was a suburb of Douala.
"They came so many that some of them forgot their travelling papers.

"Arrangements were all afoot at the Bay as the Mimbo passed. 'If you want see we go, give money first', our Douala sisters kept on saying. Bar owners are in the habit of displaying such signs. A Buea man fell victim by paying before and it was a five thousand francs note.

"He told me that he was to be given change for 3.500 francs. Just then after everybody had danced and it was well over the hand of the law fell. Those without travelling papers were given free ride and this my sister who had been paid for this service was among the lot. The money was not recovered, a search yielding nothing.

"After the interruption and break, we fell to it again. There were not many women dancing 'flesh to flesh' again. Sandy, Dave, Sammy and Henry plus their opposite numbers down here kept it up till 5 in the morning."

Chapter Six
Ako-Aya and Women: Personal Experiences

The intense illustration of certain events narrated by Ako-Aya can only be explained by the fact that he was an eye-witness to them and so could give direct evidence. This is especially so in his personal experiences with women.

Was Ako-Aya merely indulging in vivid journalism in order to sell his paper or was he truly making confessions as to his promiscuous proclivities? These are difficult questions to which answers can only be surmised, a fortiori, with a lot of hesitation. Maybe he was just telling us of the incidental advantages, albeit immoral, that flowed from his duty post as Leader of all Prostitutes.

He wrote:

i) <u>'WEDNESDAY AUGUST 4, 1971: GOING TO OKU</u>

"I got a telegram from Victoria and how can I help reproducing it here.

"'Ako Care Sammy Mukete,

"'Outlook Office,

"'KUMBA.

"'Return immediately wonderful tribalistic doings in Buea proceed immediately.

"PUBLISHER."

"As with some employers of Labour, only one's services are valued and not the person himself and how can I go back to Buea when I am on my way to cure myself at Oku.

"So with an aching back due to my imprisonment on top of the banda, I started on my way to this land.

"With my big coat I sat near the driver who insisted that payment be done before we moved. My big coat fooled him and he didn't ask me. Then we took off, this time with another driver on the steering. The mud from Bafoussam past Mbouda to Bamenda is one which needs no description. "We reached Bamenda, and I walked away cooly as if I had paid but this time not to the Highland whose Proprietor has turned to second hand car sales but to the Ringway.

"Came the evening and came these fat Bamenda beauties. There were the big stut drinking coffee Bang fen ones from Nso and the big Kiravi plus Chuku chuku beef eating ones from Wum. I settled on the Wum one and munched chuku-chuku beef like a corn grinder grinds corn.

"Mark you the Kiravi and the beef were taken on signature. Was I not wearing a coat and did I not look like a person from Buea? "As a guest I was supposed to pay all the next morning before I left. The morning brought problems - payment for services enclosed to the person from Wum and payment to the Hotel but I paid nothing to either party and what more, both the Hotel and woman were compelled to pay me money which enabled me leave next day to Oku.

ii) "FRIDAY JULY 30, 1971: IMPRISONED

"Like last time I left this sea-port without a franc in my pocket. One of these big men from overseas who tie head-ties around their heads gave me a lift to Kumba.

Chapter Six: Ako-Aya and Women - Personal Experiences

"The place is cleaned of its grass and several people in this bustling town connecting elec-tricity to their houses. So my last visit to this town brought some improvement.

"Well, I had to sleep in this town in order to continue my journey the next day. The deadly disease is all over me and I lived on fluids rather than on solid food. No wonder Europeans were dying like rats when malaria struck. I taxied to see a friend near the G.T.C. in Fiango, when by the side a girl selling oranges caught my fancy.

"Though dressed, she was a pearl of beauty. She told me that she stays with her father but that the man comes home drunk every night and will not notice us. But as is usual with me, this is the one night the man came home sober. He had been refused credit for this time.

"He pounded on the door and there was no 'Bottom bed' because I was lying on a mat; as there were no way to hide my last resort was to climb up the 'Banda', this is where he dries his corn. The whole place up there was very dark and I was virtually imprisoned in a dungeon.

"He walked in with a snarl on his face -its the local one room type of house, the room serving as kitchen, sleeping room, eating room. He chose only this time of night to roast corn and lighting a fire he climbed up the 'bands' to get some really dry corn. My heart missed several beats that I would be discovered, but for once I was not. The smoke almost blinded me.

"The following day it rained the whole day and he kept in doors and I was up there in prison.

"It was only last evening that he went out to drink and I walked out of that house - prison more dead than alive.

"Gregory and its effect will have to wait my arrival from Oku where I leave today from Kumba."

iii) "TUESDAY OCT. 5, 1971: WEEK-END RETURNS"

"I am not going to write about the President's visit on Saturday. I am not going even to write about Sunday's activities and the wonderful oration given the Head of State and his former and present vices, I am going to write about just those things that gladden my heart.
"The long week-end started on Thursday, the last day of the month. I went to this Atlantic Bis and was downing my usual 'espe.' Then some body came to me to say my girl-friend who has become my wife was wanted up in Buea to serve guests. Knowing this Buea people and their konny I decided to take her up. Came Friday the 1st and we all went to the centenary stadium, where I was happy to watch the chief of my village being decorated. In the evening the 'Be' was being opened, and you may think the swindling story a few months back would have discouraged the Ibos in this their wanton display of wealth. An Ibo chap was engaged in a heart to heart talk at the Bay and he bought 21 Beck for the two sisters and 3.000 francs to 'chop big day.' I alternated between the 'Be' and the Limbe River Club where free drinks flowed in honour of '33' night.

"On Saturday, I climbed up where I remained till yesterday afternoon. The rains on Saturday robbed me of seeing the President drive through, then on Saturday, I thought I was standing by the Washington memorial as I watched a similarity of the Negros match on Washington. This time it was Cameroonians matching for joy on President Ahidjo.

"Saturday evening found me in Buea and I went to find out where my G.F. was staying. A Buea Hospital man

Chapter Six: Ako-Aya and Women - Personal Experiences

must have seen her and paid her a visit. I watched him knock the house for two hours; then his wife left the Clerk quarters and caught him tapping at the window in the back then a fight ensured 'weti you di do here' each asked the other.

"Buea with its cold has no mosquito and equally has no women and every woman here has a husband or a permanent boy friend. Folks like us found it a 2 day difficult stay.
"'Me too ah been mars', those I met told me with joy-joy of these ten years, the peace and pros-perity they have brought. Well the lorries that brought us up could not take us back yesterday and we slept again in Buea up till this morning.

iv)   "TUESDAY DEC. 7, 1971:
                WEEK-END RETURNS"

"When I said many people wanted Christmas clothes and chop, I did not refer to anybody in particular, I was merely decrying a general concern which need be no concern at all.

"The week-end met me on the threshold of one of these impromptu journeys up north, but my heart felt heavy, for I just heard the sad news of a ghashly accident at Matnfe so I decided to pass through Mamfe, accident or no accident. "But before pushing off I took a trip to Tiko, to start the week-end and there, goodluck for me I met one of these beauties.

"She told me that her C.P. was 500 francs and who was I to refuse when at Victoria the standard price was 5.000 francs recently gone down to 1.000 francs due to a fall in business.

"Later, I had scarcely rounded up fully when she jumped up and told me 'your money dong finish, lef me ah go.'

But when she looked the will of a CDC worker at her immaculate white on pay day, lest you loose dress and saw red, she jumped at my neck and I thought she would scratch out my eyes, 'you go give me you pay, moni deh', 5,000 francs now, you dong put me sick.'

"I nearly died of fright so I took to my heels and what did I hear but 'Catcham, catcham tifman tifman.'
"A stone then another followed, I fell and the next thing was hands and sticks beating my brains out.

"I hear it was no 'stick' but only her 'flower', I am back to Victoria with a sour face and swollen head, but I won't say anything until I have told you about these CDC camps in Tiko on pay day.
"I scarcely think of my pay because it comes so naturally these days that I have started developing a big belly and my Publisher says it is no one's pride but his.

"But this thing they call pay day in CDC Camps is like the annual feast of 'Nkambe' in Mamfe where people feast hard.

"I dared not push my head out of my hiding in the camp and in every home in the camp husband and wives were very busy checking and recon-ciling, accounts, 'Mukanjo sixty, Mbonga, thirty-five , Kanda cow twenty' and so on until you begin to wonder whether calculating machines are more accurate than these CDC camp men. Dare not go against the will of a CDC worker on pay day, lest you loose your head. With three thousand francs your life is threatened with 'I kill you a pay moni deh.'

"Their girls are very moderate and refuse to make themselves bear any similarity with camp life. But with cows grazing in the surrounding shrubs, it is only suggestive of the approach of Christmas.
"Massa I wan new close."

Chapter Six: Ako-Aya and Women - Personal Experiences

v)   "FRIDAY OCT. 7, 1971:
                NKANNE DONG BURN

"I may well have said Church Street dong burn because Nkanne in Douala and Church Street in Victoria or Ibo Quarters at Fiango in Kumba, not to talk of Abakwa in Bamenda all perform the same functions. The only trouble however is that the Douala own was razed. High flames went up to high heaven as if in sacrifice.

"So caterpillars and bud-dozers now steam around over what used to be known as Nkanne. I am not saying that Church Street should be razed. "But you know I had been brought up by my master not to receive or take bribe. These days I find that I am bound to give if I want to succeed in any thing. Its not only when you want a job or money or forwarding your papers. Its gone further than that.
"In the capital from where I am writing you must bribe a B/F before she agrees to go. The bribe takes the form of drinks and some times food. This is how it all happened. I was staying at the Central Hotel and arranged for one to be brought up, she came with a B/F and insisted that, I pass him drink before we go.

"I am sure I have confused you with he and she. You see my friend told his messenger that whenever he was bringing news from his girl-friend she should be spoken of as 'He.'

"On one of these market days when wives and G/F'S file into offices the messenger-boy came in, my friend was sitting with his wife. 'What did you find him doing my friend asked said the messenger boy, I found him plaiting his hair Sir'.

"The wife caught the trick and a fight ensued. "But back to the Capital, I wish somebody to tell me whether I am white or black. You see each time I enter my office here the clerks say in French 'What does this Englishman want.' I like to say that while I may be English speaking I am not an English man.

"But you must pity my poor face and hands. The journey from Diwalla to the capital took 5 days for no reason explained to me, the train stopped for 2 days."

vi)   "<u>WEDNESDAY</u> OCT. 27, 1971: MAMMY <u>WATER</u>

"And Victoria was in darkness' this is not Genesis and its creation story, this is our power Company disconnecting current from our industries and entertainment spots, no matter whether they owe you or not, Bekoko's word is law. No current, no light no work, massive unemployment. Good for a developing country, good for a company that should stimulate industries. Our one consolation is that Bekoko will also eventually swell the ranks of those this company dismisses, we will then hear him pipe in another fashion.

"But in this darkness, in this entertainment spot current having been cut and by candle light I meet her and, her 'branch' was 'Gold Half.' Over two we decided to go home, but I had spent all my money in this joint and there was nothing left in my pocket. After about an hour she told me she was going but you know the usual trick 'come and see me in my office tomorrow.' I went to see her off and on my return I found a coffin on my bed. I shouted but no neighbours came. I must have swooned, because when I woke in the morning the coffin was still there.

"My friends came into the room and saw nothing but the coffin was there surely in front of me, I was advised to put what amount I considered proper on the coffin, I did so and the following day the coffin disappeared.

Chapter Six: *Ako-Aya and Women - Personal Experiences*

"This mammy water thing is becoming very rampant nowadays. Formerly I heard if you were friends you could either get money or riches but these days they are out to kill.

"Brother these days if you do not know a woman during the day do not take her to your house at night, you will only be putting the last nail over your coffin."

vii)   "WEDNESDAY SEPT. 19, 1973: KUMBA SO SO SLEEP"

"So the last week-end found me in Texas ville, as they call Kumba. Also heading for Kumba were members of my armed forces from all over the world, I mean those from this bilingual village. They numbered up to hong at the meeting place. "I wondered who is enforcing this new law as my queens duly held their meeting in the customary court building and surely with an official permit.

"One of them told me 'we gofmen trong pass mark man we i no cam for meeting i di pay 3 crate beer.'
I went after my own business which carried me right to3 Corner and would you believe it that I got stranded at the end by 12 mid night.
"All night clubs had closed for one day, the tansif taxis were not there and every place looked dead.

"It looked funny to see a busy town like Kumba dead by mid night. I asked one of the Police men who filled the streets after mid night as I shuffled along on foot on my 3 mile journey back to Kumba town and he told me 'you no sabi say state of emergency dis?'

"I thought I was in a different state and not in a Cameroonian town. With all its competition I think Kumba will soon become the number one ghost town in the South West Province unless the new boss does something about it.

"Then about my story last issue I noticed eight people reading one newspaper. Four had to stoop down in order to read from below.

"It is not that the money to pay 50 frs. a drop for taxi is not there or 20 frs to buy a paper, it is because 'na so we been dey before.'

"Do not get me wrong, the North West is a Province after my heart, where else is Oku situated or the Bali long necks or the coffee ban fens with their big stont, the latest additions are Mentchoum and Batibo beauties who migrate from the rural areas to Mankon.

"By the way I am writing this from my hotel room at the 'ling-way' on my way to Oku. My visit to Oku is not because of any malaria.

"I have been stricken by a more deadly disease - that called 'Franclessness' which has afflicted me and I go to consult the gods. 'Many people from the deep South in pretext of 'going on tours' .have recently been going to Oku. In my next issue I am going to tell you those I saw and why they went to Oku."

Chapter Seven

Ako-Aya and Gossips

It was said of Ako-Aya that he was omnipresent. Hence the belief that he could uncover any story, be they events that happened in the darkness of the night. All these were subsequently exposed the following week in his column. The result was that, one had to do a U-turn, before indulging in any mischievous activity, for fear that Ako-Aya was watching. Indeed, he genuinely played the role of BIG BROTHER in George Orwell's 1984.

The stories which follow are satires.

He wrote:

i) "FRIDAY AUGUST 6, 1971: RETURNING HOME

"I was ready to leave yesterday morning when the Hotel delivered another telegram to me threatening that if I didn't return, I would be sacked. Moreover whether it is the Bamenda air or not I got up feeling very well no sweating, no weakness, no dizziness, no head ache, no loss of appetite – just myself as sound as a bell. Thirdly, I hear some churches have been holding their conventions and synod meetings in Oku and this may have an adverse effect on the healing water of the lake.

"so whatever is happening down the coast – in Buea, Tiko, Victoria and Kumba that is me coming. I hear a former teacher turned forestman helped along by his 'Chaingo' has fallen within the warm embrace of the law and pretends to have had a motor accident when he was dancing in Black-Watch Saturday night, I hear a chief had been promoted during the days I have been away and I am coming to write about all of them 'one by one.'

"Look out for next issue."

ii) "TUESDAY AUGUST 24, 1971:
AH DI GO FOR POLICE

"When people started attacking me for being ungrateful I begin to wonder whether I shouldn't give up in 'education' the public.

"How can I be termed ungrateful when people like beautiful Miss Julsick who is attached to those big delegates of culture in Buea decided to double cross his prominent Cameroonian who is contemplating on abandoning his profession for business.

"There are times when people let their anger to overcome their reason and nobody can give judge-went on the out-come of such short out-bursts. "But the one which took place recently at Buea wasn't just a display of anger, it was a real show down.

"Two Mercedez-Benz cars were parked outside her house when the Policeman who had furnished it from Gas Cooker, Dumlopillo to the very carpet on the floor was busy inside. I couldn't help suppressing a smile when I understood that this girl had kept out of sight of the business man for almost a week simply because a 'doctor' without a hospital from overseas was around town.

"In less than twenty minutes the job was done and out came the large Vono family bed which disappeared into smoke carried away by the businessman, chairs and cushions and all the rest.

"A one-time semi-paradise was in twenty minutes transformed into a dancing hall a typical reward for ungratefulness, and as the cars drove off, lovely Miss Julsick who had no where even to sit sat down on a pillar and stared in disbelief.

Chapter Seven: Ako-Aya and Gossips

"The world is a wonderful place and can everybody still say I am ungrateful now?

"What about this woman in Gardens Victoria who decided to abandon her own house because five hefty men 'signed-die' at her door each wanting to take a turn T.D.B.
"She left her door open and told them I di go for call police and disappeared into the night.
She never came back. Can you guess where she passed the night?"

iii)   "FRIDAY AUGUST 27, 1971:
              MAN FIT DIE O

"This week has been so boring that my poor publisher decided to take me out for a trip together with another colleague A.F.D...O to Ndian Division to see the out-of-the way areas of West Cameroon, but I am not going to write anything about our trip today.

"I want to lead the search for this female boxer who is said to be at large. I cannot understand why girls have taken the upper hand in striking the men first when they know that they will eventually be the first to get a belly ful of the beating.

"Take this one at this local-joint who slapped a gentleman three times on the jaws for asking to dance with her.

"The young man merely rubbed his jaws and smiled. I admired such self control, but this girl thinking herself a Joe Frazier called another boy and slapped him for making comments about her conduct.

"Being less concerned with etiquette himself he lost no time but dealt her a blow which punctured the skin above her eyes.

"Tribalism will never end when people fail to see the right things and go blindly to support; my country girl.'

"A beefy-aimed Highways fellow, who had the built of a successful up-country wrestler bull-dozed into the scene and landed a slap on an Outlook staff man with a Moslem name who was trying to act the part of 'honest-broker.'

"These female violences don't end in Victoria; what about this beautiful Miss NCH... at this airport town who thought that the only way out of her 'pala-pala' with her man-friend was to pull at what I dare not call until he cried in paid 'man fit die o.'

"Since women have started buying men, I am beginning to feel that in the near future the country will become like that of 'Amazons' where women are the bosses and men the 'drivers' and servants."

iv) "THURSDAY SEPT. 23, 1971: BACK MY TAXI

"I have a mind to promulgate another edict forbidding the refund of money or goods from one Party to another who have either been married or had arrangements to. The other day I was around Meme, a fight ensued between people 'whe dem married I dong broke.'

"'Back my sense whe i put you for machine' the man said each word with a blow. He had appren-ticed the woman to a good seamstress and she had come out qualified and making a lot of money and left the man into a bargain.

"Take this other julsic affair in Buea for instance. The man had no right to move the property from that house, but he moved it all the same.

"Of course if you are one of those who get care-less money, you can afford to spend it in a careless way. One of those careless ways is buy a taxi and register it in the name of a girl-friend, or to send one for training overseas, or' to build a house with the plan in the name of a woman.

"The likeness between both parties never last, at least 'Ndolo' is not meant to last and one starts wanting to get these things back. I know how it hurts to give some body something and yet the person is now an enemy.

"So in Victoria and Douala, there have been frequent fights of 'Back my Taxi', 'Back my sense whe i pay you shorthand for England 'back my house.' But these immovables, the taxi has never gone back to the man and her driver still pays his daily intake 'Na this Madam I know' the taxi driver told me confidentially. As for the sense in shorthand in Britain, she has used it to get a lucrative job and the man cannot get anything back and as for the house, the rents are collected by a firm in Victoria.

"The point I am making is that we men will always be duped by women, if most of those things were done to men, the men would always remain grateful."

v) <u>"FRIDAY OCT. 8, 1971:
NA **NYUNGU**?</u>

"Wonders shall never end. From my birth, I have always mentioned that superstition is a force even though I grew up in that village where my mother, may she rest in peace, used to throw out half the cup of water she intended to drink as a libation for the great and dead ones.

"But what explanation can this big electrician give for allowing his relative who died in hospital several days ago just after the elec-tricians got a promotion, to remain in the mortuary until the corpse got so swollen that there was no coffin big enough to contain it?

"The poor dead man became more than double his size and body and only a tractor was able to carry him to New town for burial,
'This unfortunate situation intrigued so many women who must have been his customers that some kept asking as the tractor rolled by 'Na Nyungu? No bi Nyungu dis?'
'Then I went to this new Bell Hotel Saloon two days ago and I nearly jumped out of my skin when I saw ay publisher singing at the microphone.

"'This world is not my home, I am just passing through......' he drawled on."

"He passed by air this morning to Ethiopia. I am determined to follow him also by air tomorrow.

"QUESTIONA IRE

"Dear Ako-Aya,

"'If you visited your girl friend and she asked you to choose between 'Chop before sex' or sex before chop, which would you choose?

"'LATCHE S.T.
KUMBA'

"ANSWER

"'For a greeting I would ask her to kiss me first and then you know what comes next. The chop can wait.'
A. Aya.

Chapter Seven: Ako-Aya and Gossips

"Dear Ako-Aya,

"'A man, call him Mr. X. is on the brink of divorce simply because he caught his wife in a friends bed room. What advice have you for this unhappy Mr. X.?

"'Jules A. VICTORIA'

"ANSWER

"'If the friend is married, let Mr. X. take his own wife too to his bedroom, stay there with her and see what his wife will say when she returns. They may get reconciled.
"'If the friend is not married he must have a girl friend.

"'A. Aya.'

"Dear Ako-Aya,

"'I am married and my junior brother is staying with me, but he expects my wife to respect him equally as she respects me, the husband. Is this practicable?

"'Gustave VICTORIA'

"ANSWER

"'Fear that your brother, because he can seize your wife even before you die. He seems to love her, that he behaves as though both of you are married to her.

"'A. Aya.'

"Dear Ako-Aya,

"'Thank you for opening questions in your column.
"Please what will happen to an employee who will refuse

extra jobs from his employer immediately after 2.30 p.m. which is the start of drinking time, since we are not allowed to drink during working hours.

"'May you also quote the edict under which this falls. ,

"'Angeh Jenior
VICTORIA'

"ANSWER

"'Edict 251 forbids working during drinking hours. That employer is a cheat and can act against you at the first confidential report. To stand on the safe side, work hard during working hours after that ride on boy.

"'A. Aya.'

"'Dear Ako-Aya,

"'What would you tell a man who advocates intertribal marriages?

"'Simon Besong
A, BUEA'

"ANSWER

If he is not from my tribe I would ask him to start by giving his sister to me.

"A. Aya."

Chapter Seven: Ako-Aya and Gossips

vi) " <u>WEDNESDAY OCT. 20, 1971:
DEM THROW STONE BACK FOR MY BED</u>

"Before I bring you the story about this beautiful Monic who taught a hefty gentleman sense by filling his bed with stones, which she threw through a hole as he was busy inside with a new arrival, I will first reply my publisher's letter. Much as I would have liked to present here the whole reply I sent to this man my heart aches at the way this man treated me.

"I know I am a wretch but need I be told and by my own Publisher that I am a serf? That I should be looked down upon?

"Well maybe Mr. Publisher is taking liberties because he is my boss.

"I will forget about all that and carry on with my work, after all, was St. Steven not stoned to death because the Jews looked down on him? "And that's the way it went with this Photo-grapher without a Studio. His Camera only sees girls and they end up in this bed.

"But this Monic beauty in Gardens Victoria decided to take a business trip to this man's house and what did she meet but this other one just acquired by the camera.

"One thing saved the couple on the bed, the door, but Atonic found a hole through which she sent the stones in quick succession.

"The couple jumped every time a stone landed on the man's 'ventre' raised for a strike and soon they gave up the game, and drove for dove under the bed. But this 'otnan palava', just like their big credit always breeds jealousy.

"What about this big Director in Victoria who went all the way to the West-End in search of his second half and when he discovered that like Atonic he was late, as somebody else had already taken over, he burst all the tyres of the man's Suzuki and stood aside to wait for them.

"Pretending he didn't know this girl the Director offered to give them a lift in his car. There he beat her until her face was swollen."

vii) "FRIDAY OCT. 29, 1971: KIAFUL FOR VICTORIA FRIENDS"

"She spat on the floor and said 'careful for this Victoria friends' I wonder what was wrong with Victoria, Buea, Kumba and Bamenda friends. I have my friends and I love them and would do anything for them.

"Of course she works for this motor company, this motor company with some Cameroon's beauties. Her friend is said to work in this bank where you help yourself and help the country.

"Several times a smart messenger in BICIC has been introduced to me as a Banker till I start wondering who is a banker. Is he a messenger or a manager who works in a Bank?

"This motor-girl told me her man is a banker and her friend is a banker and two bankers due to proximity decided to side track her. So her man did not come to the house and her friend did not come to the house and the motor-girl went to look for her man.

But since the tenth reunification anniversary, have you seen most people still wearing our Great Party's uniform to the farm, to drinking places and even to market. In fact some body in Batoke told me that he has a case in court and he will wear the uniform there 'sometime Magistrate go sorry for me if I wear this uniform.' "The truth is it hurts my soul to see some body degrade the uniform by wearing it to farms - rightly I think it should be worn during solemn occasions of the Party.

"But this motor-girl found her man's car parked besides her friend's house and knocked the door. It was bolted from within. Soon a crowd formed 'IVa my massa he motor this' she continued to shout about but within the house it was pitch darkness; Bekoko had removed the current. "'This Victoria friends, Kiaful for them' she said."

Chapter Eight

Ako-Aya and Letters to the Editor

Today, it cannot be denied that these letters were written by Ako-Aya himself. This sounds bizarre if one's attention is drawn to the fact that these letters were deemed to have been sent to Ako-Aya. How he would have loved to receive such letters, in view of the burning issues raised and the messages passed on to the public. And when nobody made the attempt, he thought it wise to play the trick personally. Indeed, it was not only through such letters to the editor that he passed on his message to the people. He had another medium, namely, 'Question Time.'

He wrote:

i) "<u>WEDNESDAY</u> AUGUST 11, 1971:
<u>HOME AGAIN</u>

"I arrived last night looking very fit. Just to 'quench my thirst' I walked into the first drinking place and saw the following notice placed at the door.

"This notice has been placed on all drinking places, and in our society they are legion. The notice has also been sent to all offices and news dissemination media. It is reproduced below for the benefit of readers."

"'OFFICIAL BAN
"'<u>Popular Edict No251 of any hotel 17/7/71</u>

"'1. By virtue of the recent ban of drinking during working hours and in consideration of the fact that drinking interferes with work and by virtue of further consideration of the fact that work also interferes with drink.

"'It is hereby decreed as follows:
"'Art. Premier
"'This decree shall henceforth be referred to as Popular decree No251 of West Cameroon. "Art.2
"Working during drinking hours is hereby strictly prohibited.
"'Art.3.

"'Drinking hours shall be defined as the period which begins one minute after the end of working hours and expires one minute before the beginning of working hours. "Art.4.

"'Any one caught working during drinking hours or inducing any one to work during drinking hours or in any manner being an accessory to the offence of the provisions of the present Popular decree shall be sentenced to a term of imprison-ment ranging from one carton of Cold heart to 1 bottle to Johnnie Walker or to a fine of two crates of Ngangi to 5 crates of swindlers shome or to both such fines and imprisonment. "This decree shall be enforced by all those who have ever been suspended with complete loss of pay from having been caught working during drinking hours.

"'All drinking fans are hereby authorised to assist the above mentioned enforcement officers in the enforcement of the popular Edict No251' "Well next issue I am dealing with those issues that caused the cutting short of my journey.

ii) "TUESDAY NOV. 20, 1073:

QUESTION TIME
"Its a long time since I brought you 'question time' and I tell you I have quite a mountain full
of them.
"Here are a few just selected at random.

Chapter Eight: Ako-Aya and Letters to the Editor

"'Question 1:
"'Dear Thomas,
"'You have always been telling us of this new scheme of things with life more abundant for every one.

"'The 'everyone' only appears to be girls. They get all the employment these days and we boys must go to the 'Green Revolution' What must we do?
"JOHANNES NJOH
YAOUNDE"

"'Dear Johannes,
"'Don't you know the girls have more to offer in return. It is true they get offered the best jobs on a platter of gold, but I tell you employ-ment is only done in this country through exami-nation I believe they pass all the examinations which is why most of them are employed.
"Yours, A.A.'

"Question 2;
"'Dear Mr. Akot
"'A woman old enough to be my mother wants me to marry her. She is also very rich. Should I
accept?
"'TGNATIOUS EBOT,
BOTA"

"'Dear Mr. Ebot,
"'By all means go ahead. You know this country is becoming like Italy where old women go for summer. Italy is famous for its 'gigolo' trade. "If you do not mind it the money she has comes from her rich other men,
"'Ako-Aya.'

"Question 3:
"'Dear Tom,
"'Why did the 'Hanseatic' land in Victoria instead of going to land in Douala. Buses had to be hired to carry tourist from Victoria to Douala.

"'AKUM JOHNS
Cassava Farms
VICTORIA'

"Dear Mr. Akum,
"'Simply because Victoria is a deep natural harbour. Douala is a creek and required frequent dredging." Ako-Aya.

"Question 4;
"'Dear Ako,
"'I hear Meme Works has been promoted to Division One. Well, the ban now lifted and the field fenced and brought into division one standard, will Kumba people learn to pay football gate-fees.
"'JOHN AKWO
KUMBA'

"Dear Mr. Akow,
"'Like you I hope some consideration will now be given the Meme population. For over ten years, Meme now has the opportunity of their team entering Division One.
"'As for improving the field, it is the Meme population to do something.
"As for paying gate-fees, they should learn to pay as well as buy newspapers.
"Ako-Aya."

Chapter Nine

Ako-Aya and his Enemies

For one who was as fearless as he was courageous, it is not surprising that Ako-Aya was not liked by every member in our society. And, of course, this group was made up of people who had been exposed for perpetrating one vice or the other - bribery, corruption, tribalism, alcoholism, prostitution, abortion, adultery and cheating. Indeed, if Ako-Aya was relentless in his efforts, it was because he took cognizance of the fact that he had enemies who were happy to hear of his ill-health and fervently hoped for his death. In addition to his article, 'WELL' of 10th February, 1971, which appeared earlier on in this book, he wrote:

i) "SATURDAY FEBRUARY 13, 1971: WELCOME ADDRESS

"I promised to bring you some titbits of my exploit in our high-society spots after my arrival from OKU.
"First of all I must tell you about my reception at the beach town which has almost become my home.
"I met my publisher in a state hardly recognizable; he was frantic I bear with anxiety over my illness.

"Many other people were worried over my illness even though I know there were many who offered candles every day that I should never return alive.

"It was this well meaning souls who organized a welcome party for me at one of these hot bars in town with very few windows. Thanks to the donations made during my illness, my publishers had quite a handsome amount to contribute to the success of the party. The tables were lined with bottles of 'becks' swindlers shome, Ngange, Meta Heineken', - I never knew there were many bottles on earth.

"I was still a little bit lazy in the head and I couldn't count how people sat behind the table, but I could make out many in the group who had been praying for my death.

"When I appeared, there were mixed shouts of 'why i no die', so so course we and Ako-Aya Oye.'

"Well readers, to run over that embarrassing moment quietly, we fell to putting down these bottles while the orchestra-boys screamed shukuma, the vocalists themselves closing their ears as they screamed to avoid getting deaf.

"Then somebody got to make me a welcome address. I don't know whether it was a man or a woman but he had a flowing 'pas d'elephant trousers and a flazing red shirt.

"He also had breats and wore artificial hair, "Dear readers I can't tell you everything said. (I think she was a girl) but she told me how happy they were when they heard that I was sick, how they had hoped and hoped that I should die. She even told me about her relationship with the lady I told you of at Bamenda and oh, what did I not hear.

"It was indeed a reception with me as guest of honour, Mr. and Mrs EW - Anthony, George the Chief and a host of others too important to name. Then it was the West End with Patricia the girl whose buttocks danced the twist when she walks serving us.

"The party at last ended and I met this beauty who couldn't make a head-way in Okoyong, but is now employed by a motor company, 'If no be this trouble I for don go for Britain', she told me in very bad pidgin English, What was the trouble.' I asked, then she blurted

Chapter Nine: Ako-Aya and his Enemies

that Mr. M had promised her secretaryship in Britain, but just when she was to leave, the man was held. 'This country dem no no people whe dem good.' How could I agree with a girl like that whose ambition is to go to Britain even if the Devil himself sends her. Well I have had invitations to also visit towns like Misanje in Donga and Mantung and Mbengwi in Momo but hou can I alone do so much work? "Perhaps an Ako-Aya's travelling fund will not be out of question."

ii) "JULY 23, 1971:
YOU GO HEAR HOT

"X always pity people who are seriously sick, especially when I visit a hospital ward and see relatives gathered around a patient's bed looking glum and sad.

"But when I announced last issue that I am set again for Oku to continue my treatment, I hear crowds of girls flocked into the Outlook Office rejoicing that I am dying for good.

"I couldn't help suppressing a smile as the grim reality of their words struck me. 'You go hear hot.'

"Whenever I write about these women who wear artificial buttocks, breast, hair, say as or about chiefs who cannot pay debts I do not have any bad intentions, I merely want to curb over Western sophistication which is fast destroying our natural beauty.

"I merely try to correct these chiefs who lower their prestige and these civil servants who cheat our government by going out to drink during official hours.

"I didn't know that my humble corrective stories hurt so much that these people want me to die of malaria.

"Well, I won't die by the grace of God and I won't stop writing too, because I am doing a service to my country.
"There are certain things which a man can't see and leave uncriticised.
"Things like these typists in government offices who can always be found sitting in swivel chairs, sleeping on their typing machines and waiting for 2.30 p.m. and these students who have taken
relentlessly to drinking in bars.
"Can their parents not find another means of entertainment for them?
"What about this big Deyoh who is threatening to oust all jobless Youths from our Central Ville – Kumba? Is that another form of employment?
"Oh this Malaria, I suppose I'll have to hurry up this driver to Oku, because, se 'I no di hear better no small.'"

Chapter Ten

Ako-Aya and the Big Towns

Although Ako-Aya was based in Victoria, he travelled extensively. This enabled him to cover interesting stories in various other towns, notably, Tiko, Buea, Kumba and Bamenda. His famous title, 'WEEK-END RETURNS', usually gave the reader a summary of the goings-on in all these towns. However, there were often occasions in which he devoted a whole article to a particular town. So in Ako-Aya's column, one got to know of the promiscuous tenden-cies of the women in Kumba, the lamentation of the people to the dusty and muddy nature of their streets following the change of seasons, and finally the high degree of tax eva-sions which understandably is the cause of the financial plight of the Kumba Urban Council. As to Tiko, he drew our attention to the 'Camp' mentality of the C.D.C. workers, the acrid stench of the Rubber Factory, and the crime wave in the fishing ports. He called the people of Buea, 'gentle-men', who were living on the past glories of a one time Capital City. Ako-Aya seemed to have liked Bamenda and so praised the industriousness of the Bamenda people, al-though he regretted the fact that the city was not blessed with an ocean and government-managed or private industries.

Before putting down the articles, Ako-Aya wrote on the various towns, I would first of all present those which summarily discussed all the towns.

He wrote:

i) "FRIDAY JULY 2, 1971:
ABOUT MANY THINGS
"I did not know that a stove was such a valuable possession till last week when in Bwinga road Tiko, this utensil was used in exchange for services rendered. A fight ensured in the early hours of the morning because payment was not forthcoming.

"One of our groups, Agi, here wants men also to gor for treatment.

"KUMBA:
"Men here are sending their wives home - 'to take the children to see their grand-dads. I hear holidays are on, the divorces are rife. A friend of mind really advocates for divorce once a year.

"VICTORIA:
"The rains are sitting in with divorces and marriages. Recent ones have been these ins-pections boss.
"More marriages in the offing, after last weeks inclusive of a chief taking on the third Race and Mbo and Lyn and Oson.
"Gregory is sky-rocketing the cost of living. "BUEA: "Chiefs here all fuming with 1819 age date of birth. Here also no divorces, just marriages planned - what with the cold and rains on M. Ndongs series of send-off's continue. I have taken purgative.

"MAMFE:
"Beautiful Miss M is to be elected at a dance tomorrow. No sanjas at this dance - let us also see the legs.

"BAMENDA:
"Good country, no problems, every body working hard with young men, their eyes down-south.
"Till next issue.'."

ii)   "TUESDAY SEPT. 28, 1971:
<u>THE WEEK-END RETURNS</u>
"The week end these days actually started from Friday afternoon with few hours on Saturday which interfere with drinking time. I first shuffled to the Atlantic Bis and the seats were entirely taken by bank people. I hear they were receiving and sending-off their West African Manager. "Came Saturday, and the pulse of the cities

Chapter Ten: Ako-Aya and the Big Towns

was beating faster and faster geamed up towards travelling of several crates. After witnessing a fight at the standard where 'woman beat man', I left for Kumba.

"There was hardly much around except a dance organised by the Sasse Old Boys resident in Kumba. This place has always shown the light as far as SOBA is concerned. Don't forget that 'Government dem be get pay' by week-end and such little money that left their hands found its way into the pubs.

"Of course, the usual Kumba beauties, the mammy wagons with big tail-boards grace the front rows of the seats. A few minutes stay and we drove off to the capital where the Prisons Club had a dance.

"I was afraid to enter the hall as the place looked like a night session of the Court of Appeal and I did not know whether their wives were witnesses or accused persons. Just like every body in the Ndian Creeks has a mosquito to net so every body in the capital has a coat, some of them, like mine from Okrika dealers. "One thing, all the women were properly dressed not the almost necked bitches that litter the streets in Victoria. Came James Brown and very few graced the dance floor, a coat is too heavy a thing to dance jerk with, the high life brought almost all.

"When next you attend a dance in Buea make sure you 'tote your own woman.' Try dancing with a woman here and it will be 'I have a biting head-ache' and of course edict 253 forbids one dancing with his boss's wife otherwise confidential reports will follow.
'By and large it was a very good dance and I did not stay long enough to watch elegant Miss Caroline Folabit elected 'Miss Prison.' I do not know whether that sends her to jail or makes her to jail or makes her a Prisons' visitor. "I came back from the capital and slept through

Sunday as my woman, elegant Miss Especiale worried me the whole evening.

iii) "THURSDAY NOV. 4, 1971: MAN NO DI KNOW

"On certain days all the bad-luck in the world befalls one and so it happened with me over the week-end. First of all this big musician from Diwala's dance did not take place. Bay Hotel is becoming quite an attraction and nobody in this sea coast town likes to dance elsewhere. "In Kumba where Anne Marie Nzie was playing, the notice clearly read 'Dress formal or traditional' and not having the formal or traditional thing, I feared for my life to go in. But it appeared this notice was only for Africans because some whites despite the notice were wearing singlets. "The rain came with a heavy down pour and this Kumba BICIC dance was not a proper success. Sunday morning and the BICIC Kumba club members, some with unwashed faces were drinking the Ngangi that was not sold.

"The Tiko affair was a real crowd-puller. If you asked as we did ask a Tiko beauty 'why you no go dance?' because some man no dey for take me' and you did take her as we did, you would be driving a bad bargain. Once inside, she is lost to you the 500 frs gate-fee notwithstanding. But it was more a meeting of planters than a dance, which was more the reason why the puller Cameroonian Artist Eboa Lot tin always chanted on top of his voice 'CDC Rubber smelling oye, smelling double.' "The music was far from that of Eboa Lottin and the Police Ban that evening which accompanied him was more military than a dance band. And so in order to look more plantation than EBOA Lottin measured the organisers of the dance, one always heard the estate managers making themselves the following question. 'How is your production coming' 'When do

Chapter Ten: Ako-Aya and the Big Towns

you expect fertilizer for my nursery.' 'Have you ordered the spares for my oil mill' etc., till you just get tired with these people who for once cannot forget about their work. My friend went in and not I because between us we had only seven 'hum' and I lingered outside.

"Even when this big Highways Rubbers directors and big civil servants think that by mere authority, it is enough to order a gentleman from his seat in a dance because he was flanked on all sides by women who count their years like Ethiopians, then we must begin to search around for other solutions other than mere pulling weight.

"The Highway boss got the worst of results. Not talk of these big blue cap men in Buea who have no pots in their houses. They have made one small Restaurant, I think they call it Restaurant ... control, their daily harbour and some of them are owing more than their two months salaries.

"But this poor Tonzon Albertwan, can do nothing to stop them they lock him up in their big coasts, at times in cells and the worst thing they have done is to threaten to demolish his Restaurant.

"Buea is such a big place, and strangers atten-ding 'conferences' as in Addis, will thank God to see a good chop house beside the road. "What of the taxi this man pays - How about his wife and children, tell me.

"But in this our ink stained job, a wife should be at the back-ground. Not this girl I am trying to get married to. With long finger nails she attacked me like a tiger does - more out of pity I left her but what of her attempt in making me like Samson - I mean by almost removing my eyes.

"As if my troubles were not sufficient, there was total blackout or as Paul says 'total eclipse' yesterday. In all these 3 places, our friends who do not wear coats were absent. I hear pay day was since twenty-second and 'something for chop sef' is not there.

"Anyway man no di know. I have recently had a barrage of questions, here are some and their answers.

"Dear Sir,
"'What is your opinion of the punishment that should be meted out to this Principal of co-educational College in Bamenda who graces his office with a vono bed.'"

iii) "TUESDAY NOV. 16, 1971: WEEK-END RETURNS AH DON GET MISSION MEDAL

"I was talking to some Cameroonian beauties over the weekend and the subject changed to marriage. It appears young men have very little chances these days marriage-wise. They said they should prefer men of 40 and over, preferably somebody who had divorced his first wife with one or two children and no sister or mother living.

"Well perennial lack of husband is a problem which must be looked into by our Economists. But while some 'cry' husbands others do not care about their husbands. Take this big CDC woman who stealthily went to visit her boy friend's sick father or this Balundu married nurse whose hus-band had to pull strings in order for her to do a nursing aid's course - there is no difference between her house and the fence in Kumba.

"So I went to Tiko again during the weekend set aside all the engagements I had in Buea. Some kind people were to keep 'kpakoko' for me but even this did not tempt me despite the fact that I went there.

Chapter Ten: Ako-Aya and the Big Towns

"I went to this Catholic Bazaar and just as I got to the gate one of these white women dressed in white from head to toe blocked my way. In a flash she pinned a decoration on my chest saying as she did so, 'Government medals maybe finished Mr. Ako-Aya and so you can't be decorated but we of the mission also see your good work. I endow you with the 1st class medal Order of Merit.

"Then I begged a ride in one of these cars where the driver connects two wires to ignite the engine and stopped over at this aviation hotel to see what the Tiko Tea time dance looks like.

"Whether that was good luck or not God alone knows but my legs carried me straight to a seat where this stores-girl-turned mistress was sitting with a bevy of subordinates.

"She brought them including this puf-puf girl, then he had to take permission from their queen Elizabeth II.

"The queen herself was an ex-student of this big college in Cross River town but she got pregnant in form two and went into hiding in idle.
"I had no trouble with the girl personally, in fact, I almost fell for her, but when she became proud and spoke to people anyhow I recoiled like a snake feeling that ugly as I am, I have better manners.

"You remember this ship that came from Bamenda with tons of garri to Tiko and sold very cheaply. The people who own Tiko market: bought this garri and after selling some of it reported to the health people and it was condemned. By this trick the Bamenda people went up and the garri was not paid for.

"This same garri was bought by other food contractors and it was not condemned. Something has to be done in this Tiko about these Ibo Taxis that 'catch' others for running during the cur-few. The injustices are becoming very apparent and where barbers become butchers or Doctors and Magistrates go down to do the work of Police men, the justice should not only be done but seen to be done.

"I shuffled to Victoria where business has become so bad that even some women by preparing for Xmas have started stealing from traders. We went to the Bell to chop river and it was full. Vocalist Ngassa was at his best. Willie and Lucy did not come - two of my new found friends and I decided to call it a day. But the usual clientele was there tankers and the rest."

v)   "TUESDAY NOV. 30, 1971: WEEK-END RETURNS

"KUMBA
"I sat inside the court and listened to a fifteen years sentence imposed on somebody. Immediately his girl-friend and mother cried so loudly that the business of the court was held up. These two women must have loved him. Note that none of his wives shed a tear, I started wondering whether in the final analysis, a girl-friend is not more loving, more sympathetic than a wife and whether a girl-friend does not stand up for one in the hour of need more than a wife, but let me hear your views on this matter.

"I shuffled to the Government Teachers Centre with its dance of the year. Nothing very special about this except that a woman, flew the Russian flag' at the dance and that one of these men who aid the courts to sentence you won the first prize at the dance. The Principal himself won 3rd prize.

Chapter Ten: Ako-Aya and the Big Towns

"The Kumba so-so stand Victim has been discharged from hospital and he is still standing. The woman is at large. This should be a lesson to those who fala other people's wives.

"BUEA
'I attended a sumptuous fund raising Buffet Luncheon Party where the donations were at least 1.000 francs. I have never touched a thousand francs for at least two years and if the good ladies know this they would not have invited me.

"Well, you know this Cinema king who runs a string of them the length and breadth of this country. He bought or was it he was sold one Ngangi - just one mark you for as little as five thousand frs.

"The good about it all is that this money is being used to help the twins and triplets and I know the money is in proper hands. "But I did not know that a mother and her daughter can be 'Mbanya.' Perhaps a Buea musician can tell us better.

"TIKO
"There are 3 people in Tiko awaiting to take my life and so I avoided the place at least I will do so for some time but I must go back. Taxi drivers I hear were very happy over the week-end as a result of the clarification of the order but some of them ask, whether the several fines they paid can be refunded or worse still what of those who couldn't pay the fines and are serving sentence for breaking an order which was misinterpreted.

"VICTORIA
"The Bay Saloon put up a special show during the week-end. They have a composition by Ngassa with a friend of mine whom I love at the strings.

"The subsequent articles were strictly dedicated to particular towns."

i) FIRST: KUMBA "TUESDAY MARCH 9, 1971: KUMBA CAM DOWN

"I sat in Kumba drinking the beer meant for special people and watched a Kumba tycoon-endeavour to buy a newspaper, He was reading the 'Times' while the vendor anxious to make 2 francs from the sale stood waiting. He gleamed through the headlines and back page and then asked for Ako-Aya. The vendor brought him the 'Outlook.' He read through the back page - smiled a bit then returned both papers to the vendor 'Nothing no day for inside' the vendor had spent twenty minutes and sold exactly nothing that time.

"This is the setting that ushered me into this fast expanding, rich but filled with an illiterate population, town, with its teaming population, banks and very fat women. Here resides people who are oblivious at their twenty-first Century right-the right to be truthfully informed.

"Well the month has only just started but 'we who are attached to Government' got our pay by the 22nd of last month. After paying off debts for services and goods rendered Kumba found the reasons for the procurement of these goods and services,

"Paying petrol off by a post-dated cheque my friend driving W.I (something) drove us to Kumba (This is a secret but we had to pay 400 francs each for petrol). At the Meme Centrale there were so many of these Victoria/Buea people, some of CDC, my friend of the constabulary, Niko of Powercam, Tom of Lands, Samuel of Bamuso and many of them others seeking refuge in Monte Carlo a week-end resort - at least for men who are broke.

Chapter Ten: Ako-Aya and the Big Towns

"I met the same group at the Kumba Club but here a few of those who call themselves Ingineers from Mboka joined us. The fat Kumba-woman - is it the

Barombi fish or the plantains that makes them fat, I do not know, any way they wiggled with their waists like 'Mbomo swallow goat', 'I am not going to recount the atrocities committed by these men on the flower of Kumba nor of the W & S (something) who was looking for a fair principal of a Training Centre (There are Teachers and Community Development Centres in Kumba) at the dead of night. I didn't even want to recall this man 'whe i die commot' in Victoria.
'But I came back by mid-day yesterday and the banks were flooded by women anxious to cash them. They all were endorsed in a neat had r/f. 'These Buea and Victoria people dem wayo' a beauty told me. I forgot I promised this two willes epidemic - read about it tomorrow."

ii) <u>"TUESDAY MARCH 23, 1971: FROM KUMBA WITH LOVE"</u>

"A few weeks ago I wrote about my visit to Kumba and since then I have been plagued with several letters saying I wrote badly about this growing economic capital. One thing I stand is truth and I know i t hurts some time to be told a few truths.
'Take this letter among several received from Kumba for instance.

'Dear Ako-Aya, I wish I knew
the meaning of your name. For African names bear some meaning. Don't speak like Shakespeare, "What is in a name." I should have told your fate in life since you have misused your golden opportunity to save your people'

"When you spoke of George who helped you that you should not die and I thought I was the person because I prayed heartily for you.

"'When again you spoke very badly about Kumbat it was like asking your mother why you were brought to this sinful world. So you have your pay.

"'Your boss is a friend to my sister: You know how things can be easy when this is concerned.
"'If you want any help come to Kumba and meet me in shade 85 B. You must write something about Kumba if you are given another chance. Bye for now.
"'GEORGE N. CHUMTAH
Kumba'"

Well, the meaning of my name is 'Let them take and cook.' You are free to interpret in any shape and form the meaning of my name, but remember that I went to Kumba last week-end. "Where did I not go to. The Meme Central purpor-ted to be runned by a Cameroonian with an Ibo man at the back-ground, the gentil with the 'services' all very fat, the 'Lido' with its exquisite music with services who beg for a bottle of 'Gold Hart.' The Authentique with its Mantronly Management. The Authentic has been 'Malified' with no female employee, even the long legged Grade.

"So I continued my journey after my usual rounds to Lobe and Ekondo Titi. This is a town or is it a village where strangers came, only at the end of the month which coincides with pay-day. It is also Ian Smith's domain where a few whites hold the teaming African population to ransom. I visited both clubs, in one I was thrown in the other I was welcome like a brother. "The council teachers here are very sure of their pay every month as the council here is very rich in the sense that there are many little amenities which they provide due

Chapter Ten: Ako-Aya and the Big Towns

to the difficult territory and this giant agriculture company kindly supplying most amenities to primary schools.

"The teachers here do not even bother to go on this 'illigal' one day sympathy strike 'we get our pay on the 20th of each month and there was no need for us to go on strike' one of the school teachers told me. I was impressed by the oil Palm Plantation owned by the entire villagers of Lobe, the sale of fruits yield so much profit to the village and aids in their development. I wish many villages could emulate this example, I came back to Kumba en route to Victoria. I predicted the next Saturday Victoria will be sieged by the Women of Kumba as everyone I saw swore Co come to Victoria 'next Saturday.' I hear there will be dances all over the place and even these people of ink-stained jobs will be sending away one of their colleagues in Buea.
"I have still not written about the ten-percent deal on contracts, but that should come up unfailingly next issue."

iii)   "FRIDAY JULY 30, 1971; IMPRISONED

"Like last time I left this sea-port without a franc in my pocket. One of these big men from overseas who tie head-ties around their heads gave me a lift to Kumba.
"The place is cleaned of its grass and several people in this bustling town connecting electri-city to their houses. So my last visit to this town brought some improvement.

"Well, I had to sleep in this town in order to continue my journey the next day. The deadly disease is all over me and I lived on fluids rather than on solid food. No wonder Europeans were dying like rats when malaria struck. I taxied to see a friend near the G.T.C. in Fiango, when by the side a girl selling oranges caught my fancy.

"Though dressed, she was a pearl of beauty. She told me that she stays with her father but that the man comes home drunk every night and will not notice us. But as is usual with me, this is the one nigh t the man came home sober. He had been refused credit for this time.

"He pounded on the door and there was no 'Bottom bed' because I was lying on a mat, as there were no way to hide, my last resort was to climb up the 'Banda', this is where he dries his corn. The whole place up there was very dark and I was virtually imprisoned in a dungeon.

"He walked in with a snarl on his face -its the local one room type of house, the room serving as kitchen, sleeping room, eating room. He chose only this time of the night, to roast' corn and lighting a fire he climbed up the 'banda' to get some really dry corn. My heart missed several beats that I would be discovered, but for once I was not. The smoke almost blinded me. "The following day it rained the whole day and he kept in-doors and I was up there in prison.

"It was only last evening that he went out to drink and I walked out of that house - prison more dead than alive.

"Gregory and its effect with will have to wait my arrival from Oku where I leave today from Kumba."

iv) "FRIDAY MAY 14, 1971; NA GIRL FRIEND OR NA MONEY-FRIEND?

"This my girl friend i like me-eh' one of my many illiterate friends told me the other day. My friend is a 'delicate tycoon' engaged in all sorts of business. He always likes to be flattered and it was to impress me that he tagged me along.

"I hate to speak about the expensive food, the heavy furnishings and the amount of money that had exchanged hands and yet my friend is uglier than myself. What did she see in him - money of course. I think the name should be changed to money-friend and not girl-friend.

"Last evening saw me in Kumba. Three lepers have come all the way from Yaounde to earn a living in Kumba by blowing an accordeon. They are hand-less and feetless and the trio dance on their buttocks whilst sitting. I grudgingly gave them 'fifty' not because I like this negligence of the Kumba Health Authorities or the kindness of Dr. Musenja who has provided them with rooms near Nako Pharmacy but because I pity the men them-selves.

"Authentique, Lido, Meme Centrale, and Gentil provided the usual amusements. In Kumba unlike other places girls come into pubs, sit down and are served with glasses but they do not buy the drinks. Any body taking them for a dance, orders a drink for them thereafter.
"And then she, stately looking, flashing a pair of very white teeth told me 'I will come' but did she come? Read about this strange experience of mine next issue."

v)   "<u>WEDNESDAY</u> NOV. 17, 1971
               <u>KUMBA SO SO STAND</u>

"Even though I hardly go to church, I still sub-scribe to the Bible and the ten commandments. That is why I praise this country for making the breaking of the 6th Commandment not only some-thing against the laws of the church but also against the people. But how many of us have the fear of God and the people at heart. How many of us do not fear people's wives and how many of us arrange secret meetings. So one of these big people enticed my friend's wife and married her whilst he was studying in the United Kingdom. What of this other one who took his friend's wife because he was jobless.

"But as they say, all day for Tif man, one day for man whe i get farm. So the hammer fell in Kumba. If you are of course married to a beauti-ful wife, you must find some mengang to protect yourself. So this man in Kumba because there was some body and a friend of his for that matter after his wife he got some 'mengang.'

"The friend did his usual injustice and the 'mengang' held him - 'he did so-so stand' now. I asked last time that one has to be kiaful with Victoria friends - this time one has to be doubly kiaful with Kumba friends.

"So I went to the Kumba hospital to find this man who cannot wear a 'dross' now. He put on Yausa clothes and looked like a tnoslem. He had not heeded the warnings given by the husband and yet why married women when the 'Fence' and 'Ibo quarter' abound with women.

"They say cheap things are dear at the end and if he had only paid one ho - he should not have had this trouble."

"QUESTION TIME
"'Dear Mr. Ako-Aya,
"'Should I get married to a slim or a fat girl I love two so much.
"'John N.
Three-Corner Kumba'

"Why don't you get married to the two then you will only have two more to get married.
"'A.Aya"

"'Dear Tom,
"'Whet advice would you give to a motorist who drives fast?
"'Whisky
VICTORIA'"

"'Dear Whisky,
"'All I would say is better to be late than be of late when driving.
"A.AYA"

"'Dear Mr. Aya,
"'Are you and the Publisher of the Outlook one Person?
"'Edward Ako VICTORIA'"

"Dear Mr. Ako,
"One in what sense?
'A. Aya

vi) <u>"FRIDAY 19, 1971:
AT THE KUMBA FAIR</u>

"'I married two woman' 'I no fit give you pass 500.' At one of the many hotels that litter this municipality, a Bakossi Pamol man was imprisoned by a Yaounde woman. The man was unable to pay fully for services rendered and he was imprisoned in the hotel room by the woman. The woman was claiming 200 francs for these services, but the man shouted 'I married two woman etc., but what was he wanting there if he has two wives, and why had the fees increased - but before I could find out, I was whisked to Kumba for this Agric show.

"So of course, the CDC stand was the greatest and as usual Tole Tea was served at the blaze of sun. It was at this time when the show was on that a bald headed Bkundu officer working in Buea but visiting Kumba was castrated by his wife, to be who is a council teacher turned surgeon.

"I visited all the stands, and Kumba - a predomi-nantly agricultural Division put forth its best during this Agric show. There were 14 hand plantains on display and of course known for its fat women, they did not allow you see clearly.

"Came lunch time to which those of us big men with coats were invited and either by accident or design no spoons were served and if you were not fast you would go hungry. So we started at it but those not invited gate crashed and seized all the food from us. Of course my beautiful coats, except that it's torn at the back was messed up with rice and egusi stew.

"Of course the dances started off, mostly earlier by the bandboys themselves. Later on Party Officials and Delegates came in free. All in all up to 30 people paid. Of course the usual Kumba clientele was there.
"If you must visit Kumba, it is best done at week-ends, they are terrible up there during week days the Agric show notwithstanding."

vii)   'SATURDAY SEPT. 21, 1974: FOR KUMBA FOR CRY MASSA

With shaven hair a good tailored maxi dress and a black bow pinned gingerly on her chest she walked gracefully to the dance floor and dug it out to the tunes of Fela in 'I be lady.' But why the shaven head I asked my beautiful sister L and she merely smiled. As if she had heard my question she replied 'I did cry my massa.'

"You must by now have guessed where it happened. Where else could it happen except on this town where there are no tansif taxis after eight for even time, this town where a store has now been put on 'another for this secretariat for we party this 'so-so tanap', and 'competition' town -Kumba.

Chapter Ten: Ako-Aya and the Big Towns

"They say money man chop fine thing but there are some money men who want to chop so much that other people cannot get even small sef. You no doubt know this Kumba druggist who must marry eight women always at a blow 3 for house and 5 for upside.

"He showed me his last find he is old enough to be her great grand father. She was to be my wife. 'Na my tycoon man' she told me 'Nyi di flow me better.'

"And it was at this grand occasion where the people who talk big gathered to celebrate their mate's second (I beg your pardon fifth) burial of his father.

"With the posh and gaily dressed ladies all giving ears to the conversation, this gent strolled with raised shoulders to this group and as he beamed at this lady and was almost winning her by smiles, his friend cut in 'my wife told me she saw you at Muea market haggling over cocoyams. How did it all end?
I bought them 'replied his friend, taken aback. "Your wife told me she could not afford them, he said with raised eye-brows. "The lady, the bone of contention winked."

i) <u>SECOND: BUEA "WEDNESDAY MARCH 31, 1971:</u> BUEA KAM UP
"I had made all arrangements to spend the week-end in Kumba. Well Kumba holds so much that is dear to me - when my publisher asked me to accompany him to this big journalist of this big news-agency to this big city of Yaounde. "Well, it was quite a grand affair with speeches after speeches and with thanks of this 'Ngange' and 'Cold Hart' darkening the tables. After, this Wembo and myself shuffled to town. I was pleased to note that Buea boasts of a new market – a carraboard market, while towns like Tiko and Mankon only have permanent block markets. 'We moved from the town

to the nature reserve and we were entertained with Kpakoko - but we were stuffed up as we had already eaten Achu at the standard.

"Around nine in the evening the cold winds intensified and I felt pains around my chest as the air heaved in and out of my chest. Even my nostrils were biting. You see my poor father died of exposure to cold and since then I had been afraid to go to Buea. Bamenda cold - yes - 'it makes you fresh but Buea cold 'di dry man blood'.

"Against my will, I was dragged to this Boundry Fund dance. At the gate they very kindly returned my three hundred francs that was all the money I had in the world. It was a well attended dance and the music was good and the girls were good. No body wore a mini but almost every body was on a Maxi - there were one or two Victorian's with sanja, otherwise every body was looking good. The band stroke and Wembo danced with Agi and I danced with Henry.

"'Buy me cold heart' a top executive of a woman asked me, but I volunteered to go buy the Gold Harp which was selling at 200 frs but she wanted me to give her the money and I refused. Presently another gentleman joined us, someone I had known several years back. He told me 'he was attached to the PM's Office. All Buea people don't work, they are attached, 'what exactly do you do?' I asked mimicking the American accent, he told me 'You know your country, since I came back I work with Mr. Ato', no Buea man works 'under' another he must always work with.

"Back to the dance I danced with Mrs. V and I hear they realised over 200 thousand profit. It is my fervent hope that this money helps those needy ones who swell our population, I met this new Hotel Director seeming very pleased with him-self. You know him, he did not ask once what a hunter should do with a gun.

"All this leaves out the 10% deal I very much wanted to write about. But I swear on my mother's grave that I will write about it on Friday."

ii) <u>"FRIDAY JAN. 21, 1972: DA CENTRE MAN CONTRI</u>

"I arrived Buea by the short road and visited the Buea General Hospital and found a woman with a gushing wound slant-wise on her face. 'Na my massa woman cut me sir' she told me amidst sobs. I climbed up further on the dusty road and saw this sign board 'for members only.' "I have said i t before in this capital city, nobody works under - it is always, I am attached to or I work with, never under. Of course they came to work with pulover and flask but the coffee or tea is served to the many b-friends and they will be working in one office. 'He has taken my G. friend because of his car' is the usual complaint.

"If there is any possessive person in Buea it is the house wife 'Ma dear you go, go dat club today the hen-pecked husband sits in after two thirty, groaning and complaining but the house wife does riot budge. Not only does she not budge but she is a green eyed monster slashing other people's faces because of her husband.

"And the girls, well its money. In Victoria you can understand the girls wanting money in order to buy dresses but in Buea they are so poorly dressed compared to their Victoria counterparts even with the men, the coats hide a week's cake of dirt on the shirts.

"But they all own plots at the layout, good a thing as they are sowing for the future. "The town is worse and perhaps needs no mention. Nobody used to good

surroundings would live there with no toilets to houses. Perhaps ... Next issue, Tiko."
THIRD: TIKO

i) TUESDAY APRIL 27, 1971: SO THIS IS TIKO?

Little did I think that even with the senior Debtors ("senior service) of COC there could be something like twenty-hungry. So when Friday eve a bricklayer in this important corporation asked us to spend the week-end with him, how could I know that he was merely trying to bleed 'Heinekens' his only choice from us, on this day. "So after this meeting where we passed a note of implicit confidence Wembo, Ben and myself made it to Tiko. As with this breed we did not fail to tail along a sister from across the Mungo with quite a good burst.

"There was a stop over at the junior service club - don't mind the class distinction in this plan-tation town - when we telephone Won - there was no reply from his house. Then this sister was annoyed and left us in disgust.
"Won still did not show up and we made our way to this town with its not only bad water supply but bad women. Nobody buys you a drink at this time 'small pay dong pass, we dey now for twenty-hungry' every body said. So we went to Cameroon Bar where a cop threatened to arrest us for entering his girl-friend's house. I told him we know the penal code inside and out and that if it was his wife we could have understood but not a girl-friend. Then to 'Summer Festival where drinks treble their prices on this opening day with as usual of all my country's musician's, this repeated initiation.

"We left and went to Muyuka where the WCNU was dancing itself and where most of the members from Victoria came ten hours late - but this is my discussion in the next issue.

Chapter Ten: Ako-Aya and the Big Towns

"Sunday morning saw us back to Tiko and this department which says it develops the Community when most of its personnel in Victoria are found drinking in bars, from 8 a.m. to 2.30 p.m. or found writing one letter - writing to prospective boy friends in this town are teaching their children to tell lies. 'Miss dong go week-end for Muyuka' a little girl told us while actually it was Mutengene where she had gone to an Assistant Swindler with 1 1/2 legs. She maintained however (of course telling lies) she slept in her house, but what can you do if a girl swears on her dead aunt.

"Up the mountain it was pay time and their long cars flooded this town. I am attached to this -you could hear them say (but I do not want to unsay what I had written before). They (the women with long sanjas) lined the verandar's in this intense heat waiting for the Mountain boys, but us from the coast hadn't the 'argent' and so we couldn't pass anything. Still they took us for the mountain rangers - what with the coats and ties on us - aftermath of the dance in Muyuka.

"If you must visit Tiko - which is the town I have been talking do so between the 3rd - 10 and 15th - 18th of each month, otherwise Matutu (rafia palm and 'Katanga' (canda cow) will both combine to give you cholera."

ii) <u>"WEDNESDAY JULY 7, 1971: THIS NEW REPUBLIC</u>

"Tiko has become the 'Republic' within a Republic at last no less a person than J.H. holds the same view. So I went to this twin party, twin in the sense that there were two parties in the same place. With a difference of six houses. "As a new 'Republic' it cuts across all accepted conventions. For example I thought a cocktail party is one where every body stands and the guests were free to mingle together, but no so in the cocktail in this new place. VIP's sat like king Arthur's knights and when heard that all the VIP's were wanted I too went. My version of VIP is very indebted persons, and knowing I owe all the banks plus Agency and Marketing Board. I thought that qualified me to take a seat. I was thrown out but looking around I saw four gentle-men like me who also owe all the banks on this side and many more on the other side of the Mungo.

"I did not grumble as this has always been so, I hear the party was thrown by the Council - well those at table had every thing and we finished off with ten of us sharing a sprite.

"The evening affairs were grander than the morning, Grander in the sense that most of the inhabitants to their joy had donated towards it. Unfortunately not all were invited and there were several fights at the entrance of non-invitees who had donated. 'I be pay fifty franc' a wan from Mondoni wept.

"Despite my writings, a lot of sawyer found its way into women's handbags and I could not help suppressing a smile as the oil dripped on several beautiful dresses.

"By and large the enthusiasm shown by the Tiko population at the birth of their 'Republic' is a pointer to the good things to come and I hope they give their administration the cooperation it deserves."

iii) "WEDNESDAY MAY 19, 1971; I WON'T LEAVE

"I am afraid I have to write about Tiko again all because there is something very special about this town. But I have always read this parable of the prodigal son to mean that wretches like us, provided we repent will be welcomed by our creator. How disappointed I was in

Chapter Ten: Ako-Aya and the Big Towns

Tiko over the week-end when a holy pastor refused to administer church services to one gone only because it is said he never went to church when living.

"Some say the holy man was correct but I hold that it was a wicked act and he should be stripped off his coat and collar.

"These days nobody wants to leave work if he can help it. Like Britain in those days they now say 'that which we have, we hold fast.'
"You remember one of these Buea based chiefs who started working before my mother was born and who count their years backwards - well he, has said.
'I won't go' and has stayed put. There is this other former Personnel Manger for this Corporation where you help yourself and your country. Law enforcement men had to bodily remove him from office. A few days ago there has been this 'I won't go' coming up again from a General Manager. Only this one owns shares in the business and it is in order to protect the interest of business that he refused to go. He's left for a while but I hear he must go back.

"As if it is only men who say 'I won't go' women are also becoming bolder and saying it too. There is this big corporation man who threw out his woman's things and a 7 weeks old baby. Think of luxury of a furnished senior service quarters, to leave this and stand pinking crumbs is what she could not bring herself to do - she too said 'I won't go' packed her things back into the house and now the man has a second woman.

"Next time the Publisher of this paper throws me out, I too will say 'I won't go' and let us see how vacancies will be created."
FOURTH; BAMENDA

i) "WEDNESDAY SEPT. 29, 1971: DEM FIT POISON MAN

"There are times like that when I decided to take trips without informing people of where I am going for fear that some of my many enemies should not lie in wait for my taxi. "So I started off in anywhere, this white 404 that goes anywhere even to the hill-tops.

"After sweating and pushing for almost half the night even though the driver took everything I had in the way of money, we arrived at this big commercial cum agricultural City of Mankon a little after midnight.

"Came Saturday and my friends were surprised to see me. These up land turban journalists are a hard working lot, for they had worked out our ration at the party to follow the ACOSCA meeting already and before I knew where J was the big man from Buea bad finished reciting his speech and Ngani after Ngani found its way down my dry throat.

"If you ever found yourself in Bamenda and you hear of a Co-operative send-off, cocktail or reception don't fail to attend because many there present a sample of every product they have or that their money can buy, and when you go there make sure you wear a long gown so that you can visit the table as many times as possible without being noted because, everybody in this town wears a gown.

"I thought the place was simply wonderful until I went into this local joint that has the same name as our Independence.
'Together with laddy and Eddy we went to see some of these up land beauties and I tell you, I nearly sent down my resignation to settle down in this town if I didn't

Chapter Ten: Ako-Aya and the Big Towns

realise that the girls were only good as show pieces, but down, down, there as James Brown said it, they were worse than logs.

"But one thing I forced myself to ignore in this place kept coming up in my mind and I felt I would burst if I didn't ask.

"Why does every body here drink only from a bottle instead of using glasses?' I burst out.

"A plumpy wench wearing a maxi or was it a midi and a black afro-wig looked at me as though I was the devil himself and my friend answered almost immediately "dem fit poison man for dis kin place.

"That sounded absurd, as I have been leaving my glass in Bay Hotel down South and running to Premier Bar for another appointment only to come back and meet it intact.

"I think it is this too much of everything chop, mimbo, women, land and land disputes that causes such a behaviour as poisoning to take root.

"Left to me, any body caught poisoning another should be punished by trying his own poison on him too.
"But my upland tour would hardly be complete if I forget to mention this big proprietor tycoon who settles bills very fast. He's not an M.P. but behaves more sophisticated than one. He bullied me out of my own trousers for talking business on Sunday and made the beer he gave us after that 'i no sweet for mop.'

"All the same I praise his efforts to settle
bills on time.

"Everywhere I went in this town people talked about nothing but this new college without a site. 'Boh i hear for radio say Mr. S. Thomas i college i dong get approval.' I thought I heard that a certain big man in Buea announced after he took office that no new school should operate this year.

"There must have been a mistake even though I saw the Land rover which St. Thomas had loaded with fowls and goats returning empty from Buea.
"I always like to mind my own business unless I see something bad that might affect the smooth running of our country.

"But what about this up-station grand journalist who thought that the best way to pay back the food a sister provides is to secure her a customer. It actually rained to this out-of-the-way quarters and before I saw three cranky faced 'angels' coming into the house, he asked me to make a choice. I told him my church was especiale and apparently he didn't hear me, but went on right ahead to make the price for night's do.

"He put it at four hundred francs and I had no objection because down the south they take 2.000 francs.
"What with my long tiring journey the evening before and especiale and Ngangi and Mbu my kind colleagues struggled to give me.

"I fell deep asleep as soon as my head touched the pillow.

"A few more days in this town and I would have refused to come back, but an old sage said business before pleasure and so came Monday and Ami de Confiance carrying a load of V.I.P.s screamed past Nkong to Victoria.

"With V.I.P. 's it is very easy to pass road barriers even after six p.m. but poor me, Law officer collared that driver at Mutengene after we had left the VIP Fon at Buea and Meme going down to Victoria and I had to continue the rest of the journey on foot. Thanks to the kind Peugeot dealers I got another one to take me home."

ii)   <u>"WEDNESDAY NOV. 10, 1971:</u>
      <u>AH FIT TRY THIS CASE FOR MANKON?</u>

"It has never been my intention to take people to court, though as one of this very big upland lawyer said sometimes that 'Justice delayed is Justice denied.' So my brains continue aching over this problem since my return from an impromptu visit up land.

"I had hardly jumped out of my taxi when a student of this school named after me St. 'Thomas' even though I'm not a 'Saint' ran to me 'sir I'm en route to Douala for glasses as our Class-room has neither light nor ventilation, one has to strain ones eyes every-day to see the chalk on the board which has caused my eyes to be bad'.

"I never hear and believe things without seeing for myself. So I was directed to a would be mimbo or eating house near a Cinema building. 'Heaven have mercy', t-i I saw the windows of this so call St. T. College sealed with rusted, corrugated iron sheets and some with kwarakwara (Bambo mat). There was no board to let people know it is a school, the doors in fact were sealed like the walls of a prison camp though I managed to peep in through one of the holes and saw only three boys sitting with bent heads plus this en-route to Douala totalling '4.'

"I never like to meddle in people's business but what of this stark printer in shrinking kabbah who will never buy a husband but finds pleasure in heaving our paper men at gates. I hear she's planning jail on these up-land paper boys for writing the simple truth.

"So I left for this big occasion at Ntamulong church where I mistook a parade of Pastors for Lawyers. I almost feared the gate to heaven was open and I way be heaved out for not repeating my visit to Oku to wash away my new old sins, but wondered if people go to heaven in black garment.

"My visit was not to attend this independence man's party tho after sleepless nights as he told me, he gave only one shot and killed three 'beep' and decided to throw a party, neither am I speaking about this lady boss who has asked all house wives to pay their taxes, nor on this big shoe man in Mankon with a long car, who ordained himself a preacher but on this occasion of the opening of this big law house in Bamenda crowned with all powers of sentencing you or we to the land of 'see no more.'

"The occasion was grand not to mention the party though not as the cooperation party where you needed a gown, for the party was only for Big gifted in quoting from section 'I' sub 'A' to chapter Mathias, and what so you expect them in? 'Black Coats.' So they were drinking during working hours contrary to edict 251.

"Even the blind could feel the bitterness in me, though I wonder if I did drink myself.

"The only body of persons that would have helped me arrest these criminals was present and drinking themselves. Lawyers, Judges, Magis-trates, Police, B.M.M., C.I.D.'s, Newspapers and Radio Reports

Chapter Ten: Ako-Aya and the Big Towns

Tankers, Politicians, Doctors, in fact all Departments were represented by their bosses even the labourers and the women's wing.

"So I came back to this town near the sea -Mountain and was angry to hear a foreigner say West Cameroon hated him. He has remained here for 40 years, is married to a Cameroonian, so I wonder what more we can give him.

"When I last wrote about 'Kiaful for Victoria 'friends', I only had half the story. I am now in possession of the other half and you can read all about it on Friday. "About this pillow for back motor, I tremble to quote the car number, it was W ...."

iii)   "TUESDAY DEC. 9, 1971: NA SO BAMENDA FINE?"

"I came up there through Mamfe but I will tell you about the goings on in Mamfe next issue. I am not going to mention the Mammy wagon 'Man no Rest' that passed through the muddy narrow road to this beautiful City Bamenda.

"I am not going to even tell you about the exploits of these men from the South who came up for the shows.

"I did not know that there were still Peace Corps (my friend calls them Peace Cups) in Cameroon till I came up. All sorts of American, Dutch, German and Swiss all doing one sort of thing or the other but doing one sure thing - building up the prosperity of Bamenda.

"Aside from Bamendakwe there is no place called Bamenda - there is now only Mezam and Mankon Town even the sign boards conspiciously leave out Bamenda. Anyway I was there and checked at the Ring way. The holes are not bad and breakfast as we have it down South, you pay for breakfast separately.

"'Boh where do you stay', a Bamenda man asks you, you then tell him 'alright I will come and buy a drink there in the evening' of course he never turns up.

"'Make one day chop no spoil my gari' a Bamenda blonde told us the following day. She had drank six harps, paid for by a Dercam chap. Then the chap asked her to go to his hotel but she mingled among the dancing groups and was later lost. So are most of the women up there very eluding at least several of the 'strangers, who came up were deceived for days on end because 'make one day chop no sport my garri',

"We moved to the tennis ball I mean ball room dance at Mankon Community Centre. First we paid, then the Honourable asked that our money be refunded. 'I no come for dance me one' a typical one will tell you 'go get permit from my massa', of course you do not know who the 'massa' is and of course you are not going to have the dance.

"Anyway to some of us, the ladies were kind-Voma and her tall elegant friend were a focent of civilisation and danced quite graciously and generally.

"About the town it self, it is bursting at the seams with development. Powercam has moved upwards giving the last touches to power supply. White stones provide good building materials and judging from those who visited the banks on Monday morning business is up and coming.

"Next issue I continue with my Bamenda visit."

v)   "<u>TUESDAY</u> DEC. 14, 1971:

                  <u>NA SO BAMENDA FINE? (2)</u>

"I received a telegramme from my Publisher asking me to come down to base. Reports of the deaths of important persons filtering through him just before Xmas have been announced.

"Well, as I said this Xmas is bringing too many complications. The wives are just bitter about it and the girl-friends have resorted to calling their mates 'lie man.' There are just too many people to please, the children with 'Xmas don come papa buy me something, the several G.F. with 'your woman sef, you fit give hi this kind small money' and of course the relatives who only ask around Xmas.

"Don't forget the schools and Colleges second term beings just after Xmas and one has to think of school fees and books.

"The Bamenda Corporative Association, a giant combine has no similarity down South and even the United Nations Development Programme has an office to help enterprises only in Pamda.

"I talked last time of the peace 'Cup' movement. There are the American ones, Dutch volunteers, Nso ones, Bali ones even Banyangi ones and German volunteers. While some help to build the place the others drink Big stut, the others being bitter and the others use fees into the bar owners.

"While the one offer service not paid for the others leave their homes to eke out an existence in Bamenda and delight in deceiving strangers 'make one day chop no trowe my garri.

"Maybe all that Bamenda needs is the sea and it will be number one town in Cameroon Occidental. Soon I am sure they will bet the sea especially that they have started digging rivers for them-selves and growing fish. I have been eating a lot of fresh fish since I came and have been going for a swim in a dug-out canoe.

"But this is unlike Mamfe, the road to the Divisional Headquarters just discourages you. I spent a night at Inland Hotel now turned to catering Rest House. The last Thursday I received a telegram from my Publisher asking me to return to base.
"He talked of very important and good people dying just before Xmas and was concerned on my behalf.

"Well, Christmas is a time when several things happen all at the same time some are good and others bad but good or bad, I will stay up here in Bamenda for some time.

"I told you how Bamenda i fine. Although Powercam are doing everything to provide electricity, are individual lighting plants and the Commercial avenue is lighted just as any other. Falling leaves from the beautiful trees and the root and the smell makes the place look as dismal as a grave. I asked for dinner at 6 p.m. and I was told 'cook don close.' Mark you I was the lone guest. Of course when I paid for my lodging I couldn't get a receipt because 'receipt book don finish.'

"Whenever you see somebody from Mamfe here in Victoria do not buy him a drink because there is no reciprocal treatment. The motor park is the only link with the out side world and the top executives wait at the park on come downs. So I found myself shaking hands with them as if I was a VIP being introduced to them. But that is where it ended shaking hands. When under 'trukang' light we met at the Apollo and Confidence the bandboys have since left none could pass the usual Espe.

Chapter Ten: Ako-Aya and the Big Towns

"When I left Bamenda, I was satisfied that here was a people determined to work hard to improve on themselves. They may grow no bananas or cocoa, but coffee fetches them all they want. Only Messrs D.E. Enow and S.T. Tataw joined 50-50 to buy me a drink in Mamfe."

Chapter Eleven

Ako-Aya and Re-Unification

The Re-unification of both East and West Cameroon brought with it several problems. The most disturbing of these problems was the drawing up of new salary scales for the civil servants in former West Cameroon. These workers had to be placed in new categories, a word which Ako-Aya later coined into 'GREGORY.' It was known that categori-sation would lead to more pay. Small wonder that many of these people were proud to declare in public places that 'My Pay Di commot For Yaounde.' The resultant inflation during this period was inevitable.

Ako-Aya wrote:

i) "FRIDAY JUNE 11, 1971:
WE VON BE FEDERAL

"I received the shock of my life when yesterday which was Ombe prize giving day, I and not either my Editor or the paper was invited. By the way my Ombe friends should know that their invitation should have read prize and not price. In our progression the editor is the number one person and all invitations should be channelled to him. Subs and columnists don't get invited unless the Editor shows the Okay.

"So we were coming back from this Buea ten-head party of principal thrown by the Delegation when we went to the city by the country house. All the teachers were there gathered reading one copy of a local News paper one of their members got from Buea. 'Money di come, we don be Federal' they told the barman who was reluctant to give them drinks on signature. He eventually gave them, what with the fear of the expulsion of his children from school either from

examination fund, harvest thanksgiving fund or one of these several funds which parents pay to enable the teachers even be able to eat.
'There was jubilation in all their hearts as they lived in dream and where to them the least teacher will be earning 50 thousand francs monthly 'like in this is.'
"But I thought chiefs were friendly to Ministers and if teachers go Federal, primary education goes Federal, there will then be no Ministry but what Cameroonians this side of the Mungo excel in, that of 'Delegate' and ergo some body lose a job but the chief told us he never said a thing like that - he had been misquoted. You see one of the unfunctions of newspapers is to 'inquote' important persons Mr. Burning/jam - you know him and Miss Jane you know her one is introvert the other extrovert.

"One loves money and needs it badly and one has too much of it and thinks nothing about it.
"Well the year started with many young people taking marriage vows. The rains have also set in with the middle-age in those about 70 also taking the plunge, muttering for better for worse, for richer not for poorer, till poverty or death do us part which ever comes earlier.

"So well do the rains provide the setting for the middle-age to get married that a garage-hand in Douala dubbing on a suit and brief-case was able for the asking wins the heart of Victoria meal they fifty year old. But a garage hand is never far from the grease and just like the leopard never loses i Cs spots, the man was spotted and the affair called off. "This is the way things are and always will be."

Chapter Eleven: Ako-Aya and Re-Unification

i) "WEDNESDAY JUNE 23, 1971:
MY PAY PI COMMOT FOR YAOUNDE

"Yesterday I visited a friend in the Capital and towards closing time he took me to town. Mark you so many people visit the banks in the capital at this time of the month and my friend had only been there a couple of days ago.

"Well, we reached the house and hardly had we sat down then the land-lord knocked saying 'Oga rent for this nous i dong reach four months, try pay me two months self.' With ejaculations my friend explained that the vehicle that was carrying their pay, was alleged lost in transit and until this vehicle was found, they could not get their pay.

"I could not help suppressing a smile – soon after a woman came to demand payment for crayfish egusi, etc., supplied during the month, and the answer was the same. Several people came in but it was always 'my pay di commot for Yaounde.'
"We then moved to a pub and he pulled out a wad of dough to buy us drinks.

"He stood me 6 bottles of especiale and bought drinks for everybody who came in.

"Buying drinks makes you popular' he confided in me. "But I told him it was better to pay debts than buying drinks for people; I in fact look on you as a foolish man if you start giving a drink to everybody, even those who earn ten times your salary.

"But and this is directed towards you, for your health's sake and for the good of your pocket, cut down gradually on your drinks."

iii) <u>"FRIDAY JUNE 25, 1971: 'GREGORY'"</u>

"The talk these days is on category or what my aunt calls 'Gregory.' You see she went to visit her son up and of course the talk was centred every evening on Gregory (category).

"Then she came down to see me and of course the talk every evening is on 'Gregory.'
"How can it be otherwise when the cost of food is gone up. Plantains, yams, and cocoyams have all tripled their price. Yet employers do not want to pay us this Gregory.

"Soon of course we will start feeling the pinch of this gregory. The cost of living is bound to go up than now and most of us are bound to be declared redundant. A situation where few people work and earn sky-high. Will the price of drinks go up, what of newspapers will they now be sold for 40 francs, what of the price of other basic needs, will a hundred francs be enough, "But I tell you the delay is driving me mad. Every body is now willing to give things on credit awaiting 'G' day. Even my land-lord has agreed that I accumulate his rents till that day. My would-be wife has advised that we don't hurry things till gregory-showing you how some of these girls can be.

"We spend all the time in offices these days working out how much we will get plus the arrears and some friends tell me of cars they will buy.

"The most talked about event these days is 'Gregory' and I hope it comes on fast enough."

iv)   **"FRIDAY JULY 16, 1971;
        <u>GREGORY NO WAN KAM?</u>**

"I hear printing presses in France are unable to cope with my printing of the money required to pay this Gregory and presses have been hired from other countries.

"It is strange how many decrees this Gregory has reached, for some of my friends i t has reached fever pitch. Everyday some of us spend hours working out how much we would expect. A friend in one of these Commercial houses is expecting the money to get married to a second wife. Another said the other day 'keep this motor sotee Gregory come.'

"But many people do not want us to get this Gregory - they talk of official translation. Can figures also be translated? The other day some big man said the translations have been sent to Geneva.

"Meanwhile as far as farmers are concerned, Gregory has come. A small bunch of plantations is now 5000 francs. What of the Post Office friends who have increased postal rates even though Gregory is yet to come and despite the fact that mails from Overseas take two days and letters from Nkambe two weeks. The cost of goods and services are going up and soon everything will surely double its price.

"But what of us who have no Gregory? I mean those who because of it have lost their jobs, well what of the displaced teachers the school leavers? I hear a big man said in Bamenda at a graduation ceremony that land is beckoning at them. How many of us can actually be farmers or how many of us can encourage our children to be farmers? More next time."

v) "FRIDAY AUGUST 13, 1971: YAOUNDE"

"1. Just after reunification Yawinde held and rightly too, a wonder place in the minds of the people. You only had to say 'I am transferred to Yawinde' and everybody will congratulate you for being lucky. Were the streets not paved with gold every body owned a car.
"2. But the place appears to have climbed down from Heaven to purgatory.
"Take my friend or is it my enemy F. who was transferred to Yawinde.

"He was so - so and so, a Personnel Manager and life nonsense. He has today moved from the place to become a Farmer. Yawinde has become the place of rest where those who were very influential in West Cameroon are transferred to knowing that however glorified those who held public offices may be, they cannot do so in perpetuity.

"Look at the last Goverrner who had an escort everywhere he went, today he is transferred to Yawinde swallowed among big shots and has paled into insignificance.
But there are others to whom the reverse is true, like this former West Cameroon AEO who in a matter of years in Yawinde has become Adviser to Administration his little French notwithstan-ding or the other AEO who now sits on a Ministerial chair.

"So whether this transfer of a chief to Yawinde is a promotion or not I leave you to judge but I know that any body transferred to Yawinde is automatically promoted. Does he not see the Minister every day?
Is his name not on the protocol list and does he not get minuted to the palace often? "And when he does visit JVest Cameroon do we not crowd around him believing every word he says, "I must also ask to be transferred to this Yawinde where most people fear to go."

Chapter Eleven: Ako-Aya and Re-Unification

vi)   <u>"THURSDAY</u> SEPT. 16, 1971: MIMBO NA NJANGI

"You know the people we call our friends t well those with whom we drink together. It does not matter if they, are men and women, Ngangi and cold heart join all of us together. "But to chagrin, it was abundantly brought clear to me that as in all things, drinking has its rules. So when a friend tells the 'sabit', 'give my friend weti him di drink' a verbal contract immediately takes place. The 'friend' is either wooing you for the day when frankaitis sets in and he cannot afford a drink for himself and looks on you to 'hip the Njangi' is 'hipping his own Njangi and thus repaying what you had given him.

"So this 'gregory' that does not want to come is killing some of us. Not only cocoyam but even Njanga have all gone up and the church street 'one - one ho' has gone up to five. The trouble is E.K. the labour Governor-General says only firms with ten people and above are obliged to pay gregory and we are 9.5 in our establishment, the half-person is my publisher's wife who works part-time. Well he is not obliged to pay 'Gregory.' Because I cannot get gregory due to the absence of this 1/2 person I cannot also 'hip Njangi' for mimbo. I am not alone in this ability to 'hip' because apart from 'Terre' no woman in this 'Cameroon accident' ever pays back. You may stand he Njangi, especial or even Beck, there is no day she can give you weme tonic sef.

"Veil I hear many women are refusing to go to Tiko these days from Victoria or Buea and the big market there is without its usual clientele. They say, that is the woman, woman fit muf belle on account of the short strip of road from Likomba to Tiko. I hope the President of this new Republic is not listening or is it not reading?

"Speaking of the muffing of the belle, the Kumba Social Court came up with the case of a man with a 404 Peugeot, this big man who looks after workers refusing to admit he had had a child with another woman before getting married to his woman tycoon. Who does not like money except myself but this tycoon woman unable to have a baby will not hear that her husband had had a child by an earlier marriage. So the man claimed that the eleven year old beautiful child's belle was muffed.

"Well, I did accompany the team of 'Outlook' reporters visited Ndian Division and beginning from tomorrow I will tell you all about the journey."

vii)   "<u>FRIDAY OCT. 22, 1971:
I PONG BI GOVERNMENT TEACHER</u>

"Sometimes I wonder how some of us big men can be callous not only to the dead but to places of worship. Did you notice how in church on Tuesday during a burial ceremony, many walked in with their hats on. How else can they show they are from Buea if they don't break with ignoring the accepted codes.

"Since my Publisher came back from Ethiopia it is always in Addis so so and so happens in Addis that in fact some of his village people say he is from 'Nteg Bokara' 'white man country' to which he agrees. Equally true are those who have just come back from Paris, New York that in London we do this prefixes every sentence till you get fed-up with the whole thing.

"So I went to Kumba a couple of days ago to look it over after such a long stay from this economic capital. The electricity chaps must be selling too much currents, judging from the number of blackouts and the dull lights that light the streets.

"We visited the pubs but there were not people around I hear it was twenty-two. We finally settled in Lido where two tables before us a lively party was certainly in progress. The Mimbo was being taken on 'trus' by some body who kept on saying 'Massa I dong be Gorment Chicha now,

"I know that some schools have been taken over by Government but I equally know that the teachers have 'not been taken over, especially that the teachers want to sue the Agencies but here was some body not sure of his next month's pay, buying drinks for a whole crowd but this was Kumba where anything way happen at any time."

viii)   "FRIDAY <u>NOV.</u> 5, 1971: <u>GREGORY I GOOD?</u>

"My friend's insurance had expired and he went to renew it. 'Beau' he said I cannot buy you an 'espe' any longer, you must go down to 'Ngangi.' He said the insurance people had increased by about 30% and to service his car, his mechanics had increased by about 20%.

"So representation came from Mammy Yayo in Fence in Kumba and from Church Street in Victoria, observers came from Buea and Tiko. The aim of this conference was to increase cost of landing charges. I didn't know by how many percent this has gone up but I hear after pay 500 francs is the least amount at any time whilst 'when moon don go' the cost will remain the same as previously and that is at 250 francs.

"So I say this Gregory thing is good and bad -good that we are all having a lot of money now even though our friends are being removed from work for 'reorganisation' but bad that we are paying more for the things we have been used to getting cheaper.

"Because of Gregory and its effects, I am constrained to make an amendment to edict 251, Art. 1

"The whole of the hours of any body's life time in Cameroon have been declared drinking hours.

Art. 1
"Only essential workers need work and by this is meant farmers and fisher men only.

Art. 3
Any body in Cameroon caught drinking during working hours, that is his life-time will be made to drink 1 1/2 times more each day.

Art. 4
"All Brewers are asked to step up production and they are to enforce this order assisted by the force as before mentioned."

Chapter Twelve

Ako-Aya and Politics

Ako-Aya wrote special articles in recognition of our National Feast Days. In the first of such articles, 'Ah GRAD PLENTY', written to coincide with one of our National Days, 1st October, he devoted much time to point out that he was strongly in favour of unification. It was also through this mechanism that he was able to level virile criticisms of the one party system and the failings of the government. All in all, he argued that the one-party system had brought peace in Cameroon.

He wrote:

i) "FRIDAY OCT. 1, 1971;
AH GRAD PLENTY

"There are few moments in my life, when happiness actually permits it. How can I be happy when daily problems mount on each other the Franc C.F.A. which is never 'there' the 'Espe' and now there is a new one Box, the rising cost of standard of living, the non-payment of gregory even though the church street fees are hitting a 'thousand.'

"But on occasions like this, I have every reason to be glad and I join the other six million of my country people in expressing happiness at this the tenth anniversary of our re-unification. "It is true of human beings that no same person surrenders certainly to hanker after uncertainly and for the Southern Cameroons at the time of Nigeria to hanker after the uncertainty of the Federal Republic of Cameroon shows with what zeal we stood for the re-unification of both territories.

"African Federations have come and gone - the Mali Federation of Senegal and French Sudan, the Ghana and Guinea Union but Cameroon Federation goes on and will go on for ever, thanks to the wisdom of our Leaders.

"The Union of French and English Oriented peoples has not been possible till Cameroon blazed the trail, in fact by the then South East Cameroon, the Cameroon Federation has been likened as a model for African Unity. This is why even though West Cameroon is only 1/5 of the population, it has played an important role in building an image around Cameroon to the outside world.

"Massa, I glad plenty for this re-unification', but my gladness can continue to permit every body, if questions like the 'warf at Victoria, a clear cut system of revenue allocation, and a bold step to further bilingualism in both states are settled to Yawinde and speak English, the folks there should be able to reply to us, no matter how badly spoken, rather than always saying 'Anglaise c'est qua' (What is English) the vigour with which French is taught in West should be the same way English is taught in the East. This way, we will really build a nation where no one is oppressed. This way, I go grad plenty."

"QUESTIONAIRE
"From next month, I will expect questions from the public. I have already received a few, like this one for instance :-

"'Dear Ako-Aya,
"'What birthday present would you like to give a business tycoon who grabs all beautiful girls?"

Chapter Twelve: Ako-Aya and Politics

ii)   "FRIDAY SEPT. 3, 1971:
                                I WEPT"

"The day was first September 1971 and the time was 12.30. I had joined those of my country-men to celebrate the 5th anniversary of the birth of our great party. Work stopped at 11 a.m. and all of us militants were supposed to go marching and rejoicing, but this edic NO25Z? The people held, and rightly too that work should not interfere with drink and of course drink with work.

"Instead of going to the field to demonstrate that we are true militants, some of us mentioned it was drinking hours. Force could not prevail and Edict N°251 was always quoted. I wept. In the capital again my tears drenched my badly sewn suit as the subversive rain started when our gallant leaders started on speeches while people drifted away leaving only women, and the rain stopped just when everybody had left. Say what you may about the CNU, as a human organisation. There are bound to be flaws but it has brought peace. It has reduced strike to a minimum and has ensured the political and economic growth of this country despite the swindlers. But the cells and branches hardly meet and even though I am a Militant and live in New Town and own a party card, still I do not know to what cell I belong - the truth is that cells don't meet and it is only the W.C.N.U. that sub-section and Elections that keep the party going. I can see a reform especially as Messrs Y.L. and I held a meeting at their cell after the Party in Ombe with Miss ... as the Secretary. Let us one and all follow this good example and adopt the motto that the cell is the basis of the Party.

"Let us be brotherly in our ways and like Julsic love our neighbours like ourselves and pack furniture from one house to another new found-ling's house. Let us welcome our friends especially like this Pastor who went to visit his flock in Church Street and not finding her in, her friends shouted 'Customer, Atuo.'"

iii)   "FRIDAY SEPT.17, 1971 MASSA I WAN
        WORK

"No sooner a Secondary School opens that all the benches are filled up and even though I have no child, yet my friends cannot pass the usual 'especial' 'Massa this moon bad, pikin dem di go for College.

"On the other hand several of the children have passed through College and for some of them their parents had to sell everything in order to pay fees. A friend of mine had to divorce his wife in order that the dowry may be refunded and so he was able to pay his son's fees. But even after College the poor parents still have to continue feeding these children because 'work, i no dey.' Not only are the children fed but as some of them have grown into manhood the parents still have to pay for their drinks at 'Bell ' hotel and for their visits to Church Street. What of payments for several fiscal stamps for appli-cations that are never answered.

"I hear a big man told some out-going students to go back to the land and work on farms. Surpri-singly, I have never seen a big man's child becoming a farmer.

"You know this new song by Eboa Lottin, about a small child in Douala, well my friend has trans-lated it to be Government should give us every-thing.

"Yes, they should give us industries so that more of our children can be employed.

"I have said nothing about girls ex-students. Eight or ten of them nowadays open up practices in the several church streets in this country. I called at one of these Chambers and saw ten girls in their late teens with two cut-and-nail beds. The beauty of Cameroon is being decorated by the cold hands of unemployment.

Chapter Twelve: Ako-Aya and Politics

"We have so many economists but like our engineers it is all cramming and passing, 'Economics is the Science which studies human behaviour etc. 'How many of them have come up with concrete proposals to reduce unemployment? "And so parents who at this time should be enjoying their 'Cold Heart' have to continue to maintain their children even after College.

"Massa, una find me work.'"

iv) "FRIDAY SEPT. 24, 1971: TEN YEARS AGO

"This country will next week be celebrating the tenth anniversary of re-unification and independence and no one can deny that there has been tremendous progress in the country these ten years. The small British - made dusty roads for their cars have been enlarged - re-unification road and the Kumba road for instance. Industries have sprung up, salaries have increased etc. etc.

"Like myself you can tell me the changes you have undergone these ten years? Ten years ago I only drank one bottle of star beer a week, today I can knock down ten especiale a day. Ten years ago I did not know what they call girl friend today, I have started a scholarship scheme and they are going to Britain one a year.
'Let me also recount what ten years have brought to some of my friends. Ten years ago he was a daily paid clerk with the defunct P.W.D., today by dint of hard-work and pluck he is a millionaire.

"Ten years ago, a Victoria 'she' was a happily married woman with a good home, today she hasn't a home and her gutted feet make her suitable only for company directors for want of better company. 'The ten years have not been favourable to some of my good friends, take this Mamfe own who was then Assistant to the Director, today he is at the bottom of the ladder, or this chief who was the first to stop for white-man house in Buea today he has reverted the Principalship of an unsecondary school up.

"By and large the years have been good as they have rolled by and we have every reason to be grateful to our creator for these years. 'Next week I am bringing you the fact that our education is going down because teachers are not being satisfied with their pay and comparing the fact that ten years ago only teachers could enter Parliament or to be Diyos, they are now engaging in other duties. Some go a hunting during school-hours, others sell in Off-Licence bars during school hours.
"But what of this anniversary celebrations? I ask that every Region should have one brewery in order to be able to cope with the great demand during this time, and I want to hear the Saturday and Monday after Friday and first of October should be all drinking days."

v)   'WEDNESDAY NOV. 24, 1971; <u>SUGGESTION TIME</u>

"As soon as I introduced question time some clever people instead of asking questions were suggesting several things. I cannot help but publish their suggestions.

"Dear Mr. Thomas,
" 'In order to be able to sell more of your papers and to get advertisements don't you think a wharf in Victoria will apart from helping you, help to improve business in West Cameroon? Don't you think business-wise all sides should be developed equally and that some industries must be sited also this side in order to create a weak link in our chain.
"JJ. Nga VICTORIA'

Chapter Twelve: Ako-Aya and Politics

"'Dear Mr. Nga,
"Your suggestions are all very good. I am sure it is not only me and my newspaper that you are thinking in relation to a wharf and industries in Victoria. As a contractor, you are also thinking that these things will give .you more contracts.
"'I also join you in suggesting that a wharf in Victoria should be a sine qua non.
"AYA."

"'Even though we hear of harmonisation yet civil servants in the East still earn more money than civil servants in the West. I suggest that for the smooth running of the Federation true harmonisation should take place. The extra money needed could come from all not only working women being made to pay taxes.
"'Please I don't want my name mentioned Dear 'We are not mentioning your name' -411 women should certainly pay tax but the taxes of those not working will definitely be paid by you and thus inflating landing charges.'

"'Dear Ako,
"I also don't want my name mentioned. My suggestion that you Mr. Ako-Aya first of all give up completely drinking your 6 bottles of your 'Espe' daily as well as collect the needed capital from Parliamentarians, top Civil Servants and 'Gregory' from CDC and Pamo employers.
"'Peter M. Buea'

"'Dear M.
'I hope you are not the legendary M" of James Bond Your suggestion is very good and I will start immediately, but to give up 6 bottles of 'Espe' is a bit hard on me.'
"LAYING A PLANTATION

"'Dear Ako,
"A plantation similar to the one owned fay Messrs Cameroon Development Corporation would require just a few milliard francs to start. If Parliamentarians gave off their extra allowances, if people. were paid extra for the jobs they do in the name of duty allowance and this allowance taken off, if we spent only half the money we spent on drinks, and those of the Private Sector off completely 'Gregory' we would get capital to start such a plantation, offer employment immediately to 18.000 people and besides sell our plantation products."

Chapter Thirteen

Ako-Aya and the Big Stories

This section of the book unfolds those big events, (especially those in Victoria) which caught the eye of every citizen. As would be expected, his literal presentation and incidental exegisis were most appealing. Hence, you would come across such interesting episodes as the fever that gripped the Victoria population when cholera struck, and the night the soldiers harassed the people in what was popularly known as 'KALE KALE.' It is equally exciting to read his version of the way the whole Victoria population was fooled in the 'Community Field' into believing that some foreign church ministers, by merely laying hands could cure the deaf, lame and dumb to name just a few ailments.

In yet another article, he called on everybody to refrain from speaking pidgin. In fact, he shocked the people when he published a letter wherein a woman had advertised her-self for marriage. Ako-Aya's version of these big stories were most interesting to read.

He wrote:

i) "FRIDAY FEB. 19, 1971: THIS KROLA DISEASE

"First it was 'Apollo' disease of the eyes, then another one and then this new one called Cholera or its called 'Krola.' Then I met this man at the bank only yesterday that he came from Mamfe and he is said not to believe the story of cholera hitting Mamfe. He said, everything there was calm and nobody died due to 'Krola.' You see I kept on worrying about my dead parents if perhaps this Krola disease would also have killed them. "Some say Guinness is the proper cure for the disease, others say special still others say Becks. Some say the inoculation helps and say, the vaccine is given free in Douala and Yaounde but in Victoria people have to buy it. As if 250 francs is not high enough the price has hit 300 frs. I believe that personal hygiene wards off an attack of the disease. Drink only boiled water. Wash your hands in warm water after toilet, keep your latrines covered, your surroun-dings clean. Avoid fresh fruits or if you must eat them they must be properly washed preferably in warm water.

"Don't ask me when I graduated in medicine because I do not, but I vent to Ofcu, and this is what the medicine man told me. You see he had told me of the disease and the Gods are angry on those Cameroonians who helped the swindlers, that is why they sent this 'krola' disease. But I forget that last time I told you I was going looking for a job from this important Corporation. My uncle wrote to me that there, such vacancies existed, applications were to be in candidate's own handwriting. Not being able to - write I begged a relation to write it for me. For school attended I put U.K. and for qualification I put, 'son of M,P..' You see my father belongs to the Mimbo Party and almost every other person's father belonged to 'Mimbo' 'Then I got a letter appointing me to this post - and to resume work in the '2' Months' time.' Next day I saw the vacancy advertised in all the papers in the world and I am merely waiting for the months in order to resume duties.

"Just the trouble with this important Corporation whose motor is not what you know but who you know."

ii) "MONDAY MAY 24, 1971; KALE KALE

"I normally sleep late but last night I slept exceptionally late. We were the usual crowd only now Paul has joined us. Just when my head touched the pillow and as we say 'sleep di sweat' I heard violent knocks at the door, "I got up and took my matchet like the Kumba BICIC man and opened the door only to find a helmeted person with a round gun in his hand. 'Go to the field' he said.

Chapter Thirteen: Ako-Aya and the Big Stories

"Everyone was going that way and so we were all gathered like good citizens willing to show our identification papers. Everybody was there and I was happy that at least for once we were all equal. The long cars left behind al though some kept jingling the keys to show that they own cars.

"I think when we shall all stand the creator's throne we shall all be equal and this is a pointer to judgement day. "In fact the least of us were quick to be served. We showed our identification papers and walked out. 'Most of those to be checked didn't care. 'I go leave here go for my house' some of them said.

"Well and so it went and banks were all closed despite the fact that there is no banking today. And of course all the schools opened late as teachers were not on in time.

"The last stung on many but that is the way things forever are and will be. There was genuine sympathy shown by others and they did everything to get it over quickly.

"Then the sun came in all its fury and beat on all of us. It is true that two women were delivered of their babies on the field.

"The aim of the Exercise is to check on 'I' cards and thus remove the undesirable from amongst us. 'My massa dong come', some of our sophisticated girls welcomed these men back, is my subject in the next issue."

iii) "WEDNESDAY DEC. 8, 1971:
API GO PRAYER FOR COMMUNITY FIELD"

"You see since I left the C.D.C. camp last week-end I have drawn one conclusion in life. That is if this profession brings ruin into my life I shall go into this neutral zone and start a new life. Why not' on some month ends I look at intermediate in the neutral zone, I have no responsibilities other than that I pay education rate justifiable because I no longer know how many children I have.

"The truth is that one of my sons at Church Street called me 'Papa Papa' last week – could I recognise him? Not until her mother whom I recognised told me: 'Nobi na da wi pickin Emmanuel weh you be give me belle for school.'

"I forced a dry smile, put my hand into my pocket and handed him a ten francs piece. Then the mother said, eh. Eh. Ako-Aya, na all moni you di givem for your picken that?' But was that my picken'?

"What of this new Church which cures people. Even these my sisters from Church Street go for prayers every afternoon 'search your minds and give your soul to God and you shall be healed of your illness.'

"I hear several people have been healed, and even 'flower' top has been healed.

"I don't like to disown people especially when they come from my own blood. But these children with 'one mother, hundred fathers' can give one a hell of trouble. "Talking about disowning people, what about these two beauties who collided in my house over the week-end?

Chapter Thirteen: Ako-Aya and the Big Stories

"They all had the same name but what could I do. I tried to stammer an introduction but one of them, stood outside and kept calling me, 'lets go now, you know I am taking part in this Miss Cold Heart beauty Contest.

"I tried to excuse myself to one of them by asking her to go home, but she drew a chair and sat down. 'Ah no di shake foot.'

"Well, I did the only thing possible in the circumstances, I locked her inside the room and went to this plosh night-club between New Town and Clerks 'Quarters.'

"The smell of sweating bodies hit me like a blow right at the gate and I managed to fight my way through the thronging crowds into the bar.
"People in Victoria like 'Awuf things and what with the mounting crates of Gold Hard and Guinness, buy one Guinness, take two or one Gold Hard and take two.'

"Almost every body including the beer got drunk while the crowded dance floor swayed right and left in the snaking curves to rhythm of super American and his new black watch Musicians."

iv)   "FRIDAY DEC. 17, 1971:
THE THIRD UNOFFICIAL LANGUAGE

I thought when our laws were being drawn up that two official languages were English and French. "After ten years of re-unification may be the laws would have but pidgin English and French as the two official languages.

"The amount of pidgin English being spoken as opposed to good English staggers the imagination.

"'Boh give me that file there' one hears language like this so rampant not only in Government offices but all over this place. I sometimes wonder why we 'humbug' G.C.E, students to have a pass in English, whereas they will come back to speak pidgin. Even in writing, pidgin still dominates as those flawless government letters of flawless minutes are no longer there. "I went to speak to one of these Douala people who held several Federal Departments in this place with the understanding that 'je parle tres bien - anglaise (I speak good English). Well as I was saying I went to speak to him over a burning issue. Please sir can you tell me why...' 'then he cut me short and said 'talk for broken English.' 'I hear dam wan fine.' I told him that I do not read pidgin English and he was amazed, so an interpreter was called to translate from his pidgin English and the English (good) that I understand. This is or are the men who claim to speak good English.

"As Christmas gets near and we are wishing each other a 'Merry Xmas as the war between husband and n-ives or B.F. and G.F. rages as to the question of 'you no buy me something for Christmas' let us be sure over one thing, that is the New year, we should speak lots of good English especially in offices and homes.

"In this fight over presents for Xmas, I advise the males to remain steadfast. If you succumb well the second school year term is only around the corner. Do not please one woman and displease your children who will be your source of help in your old age. From now till January 2nd, no more chrismit nonsense.

"Its a long time since I visited Kumba, so next issue more about Kumba and about the girl who was jilted and about so many things about Kumba."

v)   "WEDNESDAY SEPT. 4, 1974: I WAN MASSA FOR MARKET

"Every week letters keep pouring into my mail bag. Such letters sometimes are treated confiden-tially and some like this one I publish in the interest of our many readers who are in the same soup.

"Read on:

"Aya Dear,
"I am writing to you hoping that you can help me as I know no source from which I can get an address or the information I need, I am desperate.

"I am 45, working in one of these plush offices. All I want is that you Ako darling, give me suggestions of meeting men of my age and interest. I am feeling so lonely, and desperately need someone who wants me and in whom I can be interested.

"'Please would you help me by sending an address (if you know one) or by giving me some practical suggestion on what I can do. My friends are happily married and have children and are too busy with their families to bother about me.

"Signed B.S.T. VICTORIA"
"'Dear Miss B.S.T.,
"I am sorry that our policy doesn't allow us to recommend individual marriages bureaux to readers.
"'It is, I am afraid, rather difficult to give you suggestions for meeting single men of your own age. The fact is that most men of your age are not single and this is why you do not meet them in the clubs, Parties and societies which you frequent.

"'Their social life tends to be organised on a family basis rather than on an individual one. But why not make attempts with these many farmers and your office messengers.

"Dear readers,
"This is an awkward social problem which you must guard against in your youth because as it is popularly said 'a fool at forty is a fool forever.'"

vi) <u>"FRIDAY SEPT. 13, 1974: YOU TAKE THIS ONE YOU WINAM</u>

"Of all the sorrowful, saddest and stupid incidents I have witnessed in my life is one I saw in Tiko last week.

"Some gentlemen who had crossed the Mungo bridge one of them a blind man came along with three playing cards. 'You take this you winam, you take this you loss, they shouted to the curious audience.

"Somebody tried and won 50.000 frs. I learnt afterwards that he is one of them. Then came a housewife with protruding 'bobi' no doubt a nursing mother, she gaping interestingly as people were winning she tried 500 frs and won 1.000 frs. Then she tried 1.000 and lost. She lost a total of 5.000 and then she burst out crying, 'my massa go kill me today I dong loss money for school fees for nyi brother for college. There were sobs from the rest of the audience.

"What surprised me was that there were two uniformed persons besides them no doubt giving them protection. They also displayed a Minister- Order and patente.
"You can always knock me down with a feather not when I turned to the adequate page of the Penal Code and read the law against gambling.

Chapter Thirteen: Ako-Aya and the Big Stories

"First it was sugar then matches then kerosine and soon I hope it will be salt, so that we can develop the salt mines in Mamfe and when we develop, the Kumba-Mamfe-Ekok roads will be tarred so that it does not take 7 days to travel from Kumba to Mamfe due to very bad roads. "The usual sugar-kerosine shortage i boku, but salt and petrol dem finish kpata-kpata, because no vehicles could reach there. Even woman sept from Mbengwi and Bui dem no fit reach Pamda.

"Obeying the economic law of supply affecting demand, transport fare spiralled upwards. Even payment for services rendered soared because na only Bali jal dem fit reach Panda."

vii)   "OCT. 1, 1976:
THIS FRAUD MILLIONAIRESS

"Some people get rich the hard way but others prefer to feed fat on the hard earned currency of some other brethren.

"So is the case with this beer parlour woman in Church Street. One thing Kith most of those who sell in bars and off-licences is that they can easily disentangle themselves from an attempted theft or fraud charge on the contention that you the customer is drunk.

"And who would not believe a cool and calculative female fraud at a time when most of her customers are broke and want to drink O.D.

"I fell prey to this crook in Church Street. You see, as a society man, I hardly retaliate at first offence. So even when she duped me of three beer on the plausible excuse that I had taken it while I was drunk I set her a trap. She fell hopelessly. A friend had paid for a beer and left and instructing her to give it to me after I finish the one

I was on. I pretended as if I had not heard it and waited until the friend went before I asked. Of course as I guessed, she shouted, 'I beg no bring me bad luck. Nobi de beer that you di drinkam?'

"A two day old baby should have slapped me down. Even this veteran beer player whose lumpsum has been drained at Church Street to the extent that he is taking his motor bike from house to house for sale, jumped up to say she was right.

"I told him my mind and left."

viii)   "<u>FRIDAY MARCH 26, 1971</u>: <u>GOAT DI SWEET</u>

"Despite my promotion, I have been thinking what sort of job I could take if I was offered one. I would certainly not work for the CDC, not when it is reversing the hands of the clock by employing white people and snuffing away senior black ones of Mbenge. I could in those days have loved to work in Customs but the swindlers are no longer there to catch postdated cheques that bounce.

"I think the best place to work is the Price Control. How else can I not like to work there when the other day I went to visit a friend of mine who is a trader. Soon after one of these boys came in and immediately filled the table with 'Gold Hart.' Then they started talking about invoices and cost and about fines and then some fivers changed hands; I was very surprised about all such matters because I thought tribalism should be a thing of yester-years instead of growing from strength to strength. "Then I got up yesterday morning only to find out that butchers are on strike and that I would not eat meat, so this 'tiger for my belle go wake-up' Then I saw the Memorandum they submitted and they complained of being beaten always and that their meat should be sold at 300 frs per kilo. Then I think and also say, 'Goat too idi sweat.'"

ix)   "FRIDAY APRIL, 8, 1971: JAM PASS DIE MONKEY CHOP PEPPER

"It is a pity I can't continue the second half of that ten percent deal story this issue because there is some very serious problem attracting my attention now. "The pay issue is fast becoming a national phenomenon and it is more acute in West Cameroon as more and more goods are rising up agitation for pay, pay, pay.

"First is the chronic teacher problem and strike threats then the cabulco workers were chasing their Manager who was calmly enjoying life -drinking 'Cold Heart' at Mountain Hotel.

"Then at this big fishing Port town a Manager is using first to pay workers and the whole place is almost blowing up.

"I cannot understand why some of these big Managers sit on workers' hard earned Money while the poor workers are dying with wives and children at home. "Very soon the whole country will be going on strike and my God people will be buried in baskets.

"I think that's when I will die too because I eat like a horse and drink like hell ~ but when the cash is not there, 'Then How Man go Do?'

"But coming back to the money-collecting trip I made to the capital two days ago I tumbled across a damsel drinking gari with 'Makanju' (stock fish) and she nearly drained herself with it in an attempt to hide the pan when I entered the house.

"I talked to her, I wasn't surprised to hear her say 'market i don fall. How we go do now, monkey go chop pepper small time.'

"Everywhere I went people complained of 'jam jam di kill we.'

"These days in Buea girls fear to wear even trousers for fear of being arrested and taken to court the next day, they prefer to starve. My Victoria bound trip was a very funny one. Crammed up in a new roomy white, carriageless Peugeot 404 twice, I was the fifteenth passenger and she sat too close and made herself as comfortable as possible. When I asked her name she opened her big shining teeth and told me 'You think say I no sabi you?'

"She told me she was returning to Victoria to meet 'my old boy-friend' because even Buea people are not as generous as dem been tell me.' I don't sound very interesting today, I don't know why, but dare you read the next issue."

x)   "TUESDAY APRIL 20, 1971; 'IS IT NYONGO'?

"I promised you that I would continue the description of this tour to the North. How can I describe the savannah, the hurts and the stones, the town bustling with the textiles industry, the intense heat, the appolo which caught me and the girls - on the girls.

"Wrapped from head to toe in almost Indian fashion, you hardly see a girl around the towns during the day. The beauty of these girls defies description. Most of them are light-skinned with noses as long as those of hawks, a good bust and beautiful long hair. These are girls not spoilt by the Western world. In fact nature's charms come their way for the asking.

Chapter Thirteen: Ako-Aya and the Big Stories

"Think of the number of girls down south who waste money on creams in order to appear light. What of the Afro-wigs and the false bust which so much money is spent on buying. Then there is this new bra - 'under the chain' which trebles the size of bust.

"So you think she has a full bust, I mean those down-south but man, one of these days I am going to sue some body for abuse of confidence.

"These days I find it difficult to ask some body for a lift.

"I don't believe in 'iVyongo' but the young men are dying out fast whenever they cross the Mungo bridge.

"This is exactly what I was told in OKU. The trouble is we are reaching a situation in this country now where fathers are buying their sons and all because of this craze for cars, women and the roasted fish in Mungo.

"Well the girls in the North came out in the evenings in their resplendent beauty. They go for soft drinks with a whiff of something hard, eat a lot of kola, speak good pidgin English, little 151 of French and nothing of good English.

"They like to get married unlike us here whose size of your band balance determines acceptance for marriage. I fell in love with one of them and we have settled for a quiet marriage before an ESDIYO. After my marriage who knows the D.O. will be singing my name for a big post. This is the way things are."

xi)   'FRIDAY APRIL 30, 1971: AT A PARTY

"Yesterday somebody told me, at my house that my friends were waiting for me at the Kontri-man's, You know the usual group. Entering my baggy trousers I trod my way to that spot. I found the two of them, one sitting near a 'mammy' pikin another sitting near a turn-turn belle, well, you know the girls in this town, no matter their conditions they are always pining for some boy. "I sent the women off and we settled down to serious drinking. We were at it for long and only called it a day during the small hours of the morning.

"I had barely reached my house when some body handed me a blow. I know I fell down and I could feel my body being thrown into a waiting vehicle. I was gagged. The vehicle threaded its way towards man '0' War Bay and half way still gagged i was ordered down to face a group of people all with guns and knives.

"You own, too much' they all spoke at once and we will kill you they said. At a sign from the leader they pounced on me and I shouted out my top-most voice. T heard feet running towards me and woke me up. AKO-AYA na upside you sleep. I had just woken from a dreadful dream and had slept off most of the night in the centre of the highway-this was just the effect of pay-day, my friends having received their pay yesterday."

xii)   "TUESDAY AUGUST 31, 1971: MAKE WE NO WORK FOR MONDAY

"Always I am being over taken by events and I have asked that this paper be published daily but advertisers seem to be the deciding factor of how many times this is published weekly. My Ndian trip will have to wait especially the ugly fact that all Parliamentarians including the section President and Chairman of Council live away from Ndian. In fact one of them had not been home for the past 20 years.
I also accompanied these journalists to Douala and on the Ethiopian Airlines demonstrated flights. Their doing last weekend and the fact that women who do not like

Chapter Thirteen: Ako-Aya and the Big Stories

to travel with their identification papers and must collapse in hotel bathrooms will have also to wait.

"Even the fact that shops in Victoria were closed last Saturday, a series of closures this year for one reason or the other, this time because an old man instead of being allowed to spend his last days near his village is being taken up north, also not see the light of print of this issue. "What must be seen is the fact that yesterday was Monday. I visited several offices from Metne to Fako Divisions, 'Buea no bi drink this for Saturday and yesterday I not fit work something today at all' everybody was recounting. Half the day was taken with stories about the escapades of Saturday - we bean drink for Authentique' massa no be mimbo this for kit-kat, 'We left the Buea Mountain club at 4 a.m. this morning, 'Drink wan kill man for Bay yesterday.'

"On the other side of the Mungo another Brewery is coming up to join the 'Cold Heart' and 'Ngangi ones. You see the demand is greater than the supply and this brewery with its bock beer is very welcome. But will work not interfere with drink.

"This is why with so much company taxes being paid by the breweries, suggest that more be opened. I on behalf of the people of this great Republic also beg that because very little work can be done on Mondays after drinking over the week-end and since by popular decree N°251 none should interfere with the other, Mondays should be declared work free.

"I know enemies of the people will say if Monday is accepted and declared work-free, I will at a later date beg for Tuesday, then Wednesday then Thursdays then Fridays, then Saturdays and so on, if my request is granted, we may have a work-free week.

"But if we buy all the drinks produced by our breweries, we will get all the money needed from them.

"I beg to move."

xiii) "WEDNESDAY SEPT. 22, 1971: I BEEN GO FOR KATROKE CHOSS

"As I rolled uneasily in my sleep on my hard bed over the week end, I remembered those good old school days in College when Rev, Father used to force us to attend Sunday mass and I decided to go to Church for the first time since two Easters ago. So, I shuffled along Church Street in my badly sewn suit that Sunday morning to this big Church which stands between Church Street and New Town.

"Women dressed in long, long sanjas who had just dispatched their night customs, stared at me seated at the back roll of the men's column. "I don't know why men have to sit separately from women. That seems to me a sort of discrimination or separatism. I closed my eyes and fought in vain to mumble prayers to my creator but another repelling sound awoke me.

"The Church house seemed to go alive with women plastic baskets of money.

"I nudged a nearby womanshiper, one of those who passed the night at Church Street, and tried to tell him that his daughter was carried sick at midnight to the hospital while he was busy in Church Street, but he pushed one of those jingling baskets to my hand, 'Put your own offering', he whispered in my ear.

"In my honest opinion, even though the Pope might object to it, I feel that the idea of disturbing every body in Church to drop coins into baskets while the mass is

in session is very bad. Instead I would suggest that the church authorities attach collection boxes by the Church doors, so that people can be told to drop their offerings there before passing into the Church.
'During offertory, these boxes can be carried with minimum of noise to the alter. "Lest I should be thought to be biased, my week-end also carried me to other churches too.

"I peeped into this one where they cure sick people in church instead of in hospitals and the weeping I heard filled me with horror, I thought the sick man was already dead.
Coming over to the town the topic of conver-sation even up to the level of our Radio boys was about this promotion or is it an election up in Buea.

"I thought some body was trying to be subversive but a friend told me that it was the 'President' of the Bar Association that was being challenged.

"The word President brings confusion. Every small meeting has a President, every Association and every board of Directors, the word Chairman is no longer sweet in the ear because every body wants to be called President.

"But our Radio screamed a defence to that challenge aimed at levelling all the points raised.

"While the town was swinging over the week-end a miniature raid was taking place in the room of one of these Sub Editors behind this big hotel at the round about.

"The struggle arose when four girls clashed in a made scramble for two men. "A Radiogram was nearly smashed."

xiv) "THURSDAY OCT. I, 1971:
MASSA, AH WAN FOLOO YOU GO ETHIOPIA

"I usually get very irritated when people don't appreciate the good work done by others.

"All the time, I have tried to do my best to see that this paper sells and when I heard that the publisher was to go to Ethiopia on Friday, I nursed a silent hope that I would be given an opportunity to see this big Head Quarters in African politics.

"But when I walked to that his office full of windows last Wednesday and told him 'Massa ah wan follow you to Ethiopia', the man started telling me stories.

"He was rude enough to tell me that my suit is badly sewn and that Ethiopian girls don't like ugly people.

"I guess that he was implying that I am ugly. But what did I care, have I not said of enough myself that I am no angel?

"If any body can tell me off that way, I don't think for one moment that my publisher can tell me that.

"Surely he has heard about this other publisher the one who was said to be the only West Cameroonian journalist to visit Ethiopia, he really asked me to accompany him, but the Airlines people wanted only one man at a time. "There are actually three West Cameroonian journalists to go to this O.A.U. Head Country, and not one.

"All the same, I like my publisher and I have decided to go along with him, even if it means paying my own flight in this elegant plane service.

Chapter Thirteen: Ako-Aya and the Big Stories

"I will not leave my West Cameroon readers when I get to Ethiopia, I will continue to cable my stories down to Cameroon. If that is impossible my assistant will carry on until I return with a bumper from Addis.

"I told my readers I won't write about this first October day but this my girl friend who has become my wife forced me to write when she continued serving even though the guest had gone and only returned home two days after they had gone.

"When I asked her what kept her up in Buea, she started quarrelling all over the place and only cooled off after one 'espe' had changed hands.

"Next time your wife double crosses you tell her to pay a fine of one crate of 'espe' and you will be fulfilling edict 251.

"QUESTION TIME

"I told you I will be able to ensure .questions from readers and several have come in.

"QUESTION

"'Dear Ako-Aya,
"Should a short man marry a short woman and will they not deliver short children?'
"Felix F.
VICTORIA'"

"ANSWER

"'If the children are girls then problem, the shorter the better.'

"QUESTION

"'The spoken and press journalists in this country brought re-unification and its advantages to the people yet not one was decorated last Sunday, Why?

"Mr. R.F.
BUEA"

"ANSWER

"'In the toilet what do you do with the toilet roll, after you've used it. "See next issue."

xv)   "TUESDAY NOV. 9, 1971: PILLOW FOR BACK MOTOR

"Have you seen these people who place pillows at the back of their cars? They are normally different colours. I used to think that the pillows were for decorating the car, like a chaise until Saturday, when a different use was given to these pillows. In fact some of them are so faded that they decorate nothing any more.

"So while waiting to hear the usefulness of the pillows in cars why don't you come with me to the fair. It wasn't actually a fair but an agricul-tural show and but for the C.D.C. and BICIC several firms did not take part as they did last year.

"We shuffled along with the VIP's you of course know what this stands for till we got to the CDC stand. A tea chest was passed to the most important VIP but, when I asked for my own, the man there said 'we go member you other time.' 'At the Tole Tea stand you were served tea with the sun's blaze over head. A sulky American trained copy typist who attends this CDC Tiko girls Secondary Schools refused to serve us because we were

Chapter Thirteen: Ako-Aya and the Big Stories

not important but were indebted. The always drunk Secretary did not see it fit to invite any of us, to the luncheon so we went to fix ourselves lunch.

"Simon passed us the usual Espe and gol haf and his wife repeated but I can see he didn't like that. With his respect for age, he held that an old relative should have been served first before us, but we did more than pay for this at the club with 2 martels and rice and chips.

"Part-two of the show continued in the afternoon till 5 p.m. and then we found it difficult to get back. Tiko taxis stopped running at 4.30 p.m. no wonder the big market no longer sells much. The fine for breaking this rule is near fifty thousands but if you play up it can be settled. Some taxi drivers used to spy on others in the evenings and those who spy are not breaking the law, at least not in Tiko. Those who benefit from this plight of taxi drivers open their doors to harlots and the unemployed who in return act as leg-men to find them women but this is Tiko where nothing goes wrong. Well at the night we got some body to drop for money to buy petrol, then we met one of these pillow motors parked on one side of the road this time without them behind. What I saw will be the subject of tomorrow's column.

"A reader, Mr. Kuban of Cassava Farm Victoria who tells you Victoria is only made of farms has said that 'Class 7 is not better than matutu of Tiko and G.C.E, is not better than shome.'

"I wonder what he compares espe with.'

Chapter Fourteen

Ako-Aya's Problems at Job-Site

It was not always plain sailing for Ako-Aya. Indeed, he did not only have to fight against censures, but also to deal with serious administrative problems. This latter difficulty was most biting. In fact, there were months when he considered winding up the whole business. As would be recalled, a few hours before his sudden death, he had gone to see Wem, mainly to discuss the future of his paper, THE CAMEROON OUTLOOK. This disturbing part of Ako-Aya's life was made known to his readers in several ways.

He wrote:

i) "WEDNESDAY MARCH 10, 1971:
7 DAYS NOTICE"

"When I wrote about Kumba and my trip thereto, little did I know that one of the car numbers quoted belonged to my boss. Of course this morning I got a letter giving me seven days notice terminating my appointment.

"I hardly like working for another paper except this one, to beg I am not able and to steal I am ashamed and the fact that after 7 days I shall be roaming the streets looking for work scars me in the face.

"I don't know whether to take advantage of this operation Bafang thing or to be a Park Collector but after the next 7 days I will not be sure of some Especiale.

"I thought I had many sympathisers and I know I have and would ask that those who like me should plead with my boss on my behalf. Until this decision is changed how can I write in my usual style?"

ii) "FRIDAY MARCH 12, 1971-DEM DON SACK ME

"I cannot explain what led me to quote that car number, but there I have lost my job - a job that used to give some thous just when other people's pocket were dry.

"The publisher of this paper is somebody with whom it is useless to argue once he has taken a decision, and so my pleas fell on deaf ears when he told me yesterday that he has painfully decided to sack me for what he called disgracing him.

"Any way, poor me, I thought I was doing him good by helping to sell his paper with my stories but now I see I was mistaken.

"He gave me one chance though to write my last story today and stop forth with.

"So I decided to discuss this new epidemic, I mean this business of a N°2 wife.

"The law of this country says you are allowed to marry up to four wives. The church says you can marry only one and Western civilization frowns on more than one wife.

"But even this Western so-called civilised men have a trick they always employ to get more than one wife. They divorce their already married wives, get the necessary divorce certificates and then marry a fresh - but they already have children with divorced wives. So its all the same getting more than one wife.

"Today they say women, money and children are the same - the more you have the more you want to get. Gradually men, especially Cameroon men are beginning

Chapter Fourteen: Ako-Aya's Problems at Job-Site

to find out that one wife is not sufficient. They start now with mistresses then soon several times they switch over to new mistresses.

'But when mistresses start using daggers on men like this one who stays at Gardens in Victoria the men follow the usual pattern, - switch over to a new mistress.

"Then the other day I met this 'other female butcher who goes by the show naiqe 'Merecine Bascule' as if she only rides on bicycles that have medicine of first aid bags hung on them. She carried a heavy bandaged hand and I just passed quietly for fear that somewhere around her breasts, she might be carrying a knife.

I cannot count how many cases of knifing I have heard in Victoria the last one month. "Instead of people guarding against cholera these days, men still will have going about with knives in their new long gowns before talking anyhow to them.

"Readers, my heart is sour and I fear I am asking your time for nothing. I can't think straight to present any nice story to you - how can I when I have to clean my pen and hang it up after this story.

"Maybe this Outlook publisher-man will listen to readers if they appeal to him to re-employ me.

"Our big, old men enjoying comfortable office jobs say we youths should turn to the soil. I like that very much, but alas, I can only write. I will be happy if any reader can make me his or her Secretary when I lose my job.

"Expect to hear from me soon if your appeal is accepted by the Publisher, if not bye-bye."

iii)   'WEDNESDAY MARCH 17,1971;
         TODAY NA TODAY"

"Not knowing whether I am still on duty or not I shuffled once again to Kumba for week-end. Kumba is becoming the town after my own heart, what with its women and its fanless cinemas. In Kumba if you must attend films you appear to be in hell, with very fierce heat around you and with screens poorly lit.

"I came back to hear of this ten percent deal on contractors. I will tell you more about this and the 200.000 francs bribe given and taken in order to be promoted 'senior service.' I will surely not fail to write about this semi-illiterated man who apparently possesses money but heavily indebted to the Board and who addressed me 'strongly.' Well, I will write about all these if this beast of a man gives the chance."Spying on his desk there are so many fans who have written to plead on my behalf. I can see names like ASU-AYUKETANG, AG. etc.

"Take this from Jacob Ekemeloh which I stealthily removed.

"'Dear Editor,
"'I am sorry to hear of your decision to terminate Mr. Thomas Ako-Aya as a columnist in your widely read newspaper. As a constant reader of your paper, I usually read first the AKO-AYA page before any one else and I think many others do same. If you even move about with your vendors, the regular question posed to them is 'What does Ako-Aya say Today?'

"If under any condition Mr. Ako-Aya quotes a car number to your dislike I for one will recommend his being given increment as a bold worker who calls a spade a spade. Ako-Aya is a citizen who is not shading faults

Chapter Fourteen: Ako-Aya's Problems at Job-Site

because he needs daily bread and that is why we very much prefer his writings. If all citizens of this state will be very frank and behave the AKO-AYA way, I hope we shall make a great society.

"'I am making this appeal to you in good faith, to retain AKO-AYA give him an increment, good entertainment allowance and a car for his duty. But if on the contrary your decision to sack him still stands, then I will hold that your paper is only to please yourself and I will withdraw from reading it plus my many other friends.

"'You have given Mr. Ako-Aya seven days notice but the readers give you forty-eight hours to take your decision.'

"JACOB EKEMELOH Ngande Street VICTORIA"

iv)　　　　　"TUESDAY FEB. 27, 1979; I AM AN ANGRY MAN"

"Yes, I am an angry man this morning, not because I am hungry as my friends have seen me that I have a full stomach but I am angry over certain persons.

"(1) My Editor-in-Chief: You know him don't you? The one with a protruding stomach and feet whe dem bend-bend like Ayang road. Well after taking pains to write my stories he cuts some of them out or sometimes changes their meaning. He will not allow me to write about himself or his friends or his mistress.

"(2) The Privileged class: I met a prisoner the other day who told me that a member of the privileged class had stolen some goods and sold them to him. While he was serving a sentence for buying stolen property, the man who had actually stolen was still working in his office.

"They steal our tax money they misuse money sent to them for other things, they are corrupt, they take bribes, they condone smuggling but nothing happens to them, their names cannot even appear in the Outlook for doing such heinous things. The most that can happen is that they are called to adulterous functions or transferred or promoted to enable them pay the money so embezzled, but they are setting a bad example and the good book says of such people that a mile-stone should be tied round their necks and then thrown in the deepest sea. I thought the statue of Justice holds a tilted balance in one hand, a sword in the other, and eyes wide open.

"(3) A friend of mine: The other day a friend of mine who is really very vulgar went to the market to buy plantains. Now listen to this conversation:

"'Madam: how much for plantain?'

"'Woman: my plantain na one taisind.'

"'Friend: make I pay five ho.'

"'Woman: please sir pay me eight cent.'

"'Friend: your lars na how much?'

"'Woman: my lars na six hundred sir.'

"'Friend: Daso six hundred and he went, away laughing.

"Yes I am angry with such vulgar friends.

"MY VIEW

"Within a short space of six months I have lost friends in ghastly motor accidents all driven by wen. In my view, I hold that women are better drivers and accident - free.

Chapter Fourteen: Ako-Aya's Problems at Job-Site

You will argue their number driving is small than ours. Yes, and so what? Better a clean ten drivers than one million killer drivers.

"An acquaintance who suddenly got into money a few months back did so by selling two of his fine children to one famous society. This man got the whole idea of letting money serve wrong. Then he let himself to serve money. Did you know he died of an illness he would have cured with his huge sum of money? But he preferred to bank it and die.

"Once you lose the mastery of money, and you start serving money then you are in trouble. That is why the Apostle Paul was so afraid of money and made the ridiculous statement that the 'Love of money is the root of evil.' But in my view and in the view of an American Preacher, we hold that is the lock of money which is the root of all evil. I have seen more evil in the back of money than the love of it.

"But do not serve it like my Friend."

Chapter Fifteen

Ako-Aya and Misleading Titles

Ako-Aya occasionally disappointed his readers. Some of his titles were so misleading that, one had to question the mood in which he was before writing. The stories he narrated under titles such as 'NA SO BAMENDA FINE?' (3°) 'Rain Na Bad Time' and 'She Don Tif My Man', had no relationship whatsoever. This was in sharp contradiction with his attitude of generating suspense in one article, and coming out with a ready answer in the next issue. This was the case with the following articles, 'WANTED - A WIFE' and 'Woman APPLY FOR MAN'. But let us first of all look at the difficult titles.

He wrote:

i) "WEDNESDAY DEC. 15, 1971: NA SO BAMENDA FINE? (3)"

"At first my Publisher's telegram did not move me. But gradually it shook me to honour my employer. And as I told you before, that don't buy a drink for a Mamfe man because 'mimbo na Njangi' I was determined to hold my heart in Mamfe until I get down to 'Bell Hotel.' Things were actually serious, more serious than the telegramme could communicate to me. Big men were dying and other striking events made me wonder whether or not to 'enter for botro if you now wan see nonsense.'

"But with the Football in Buea and Douala, the meeting place was again at the Tiko Airport Hotel. And from every corner of the Hotel I heard those Ex-students now jobless talking of the new employment system which will henceforth guarantee the jobless with jobs, and the employer with the suitable employee and so on until I was forced to ask if new Industries will accompany this new later employment system. But all I gathered later was that in a new employment system there will

be no God father, no countriman.' Once you are qualified the job is yours.

"Then a school leaver with a dazzling blonde besides him came to me and asked: Mr. Thomas I hear we the jobless men have to register officially that we have no jobs and therefore have no source of income.

"'A ting we go free for tax.' This was however a serious question, for although many people have come to rely on my wits this question battled me enough.

"'My brother da question na for Yawinde I answer go comot.' I told him. Then a friend introduced me to a certain sexy eye miss Ap... and I fell to her knees in capitulation. I vowed for her. "And back to 'Bell Hotel I found every thing intact life moving as usual."

ii) <u>"FRIDAY NOV. 9, 1973: SHE DONG TIP MY MAN"</u>

"I sat behind the church and heard the marriage vows being taken ... 'for better for worse till poverty do us part.' Isn't that what we say when we get married.

"Then I went again to this office in the Nof Wes and met this same woman who had promised 'to have and to hold' with this young beauty - dem feet leke Cassias clay and Joe Frazier. "Before reaching the Nof West I passed by the West. I met an old Bami leke man at Mbouda learning French 'commang talevu' I said, and he replied in good French 'seven Talle Femme.' He thought I had asked him how many wives he is married to.

Chapter Fifteen: Ako-Aya and Misleading Titles

"Do not ask me why a top man should buy a blanket and leave it in an office. Well I saw this in Tiko. Do not ask me the use of blanket in an office.

"The mid-term is over and the girls and boys have returned to colleges. No one expects bloated stomachs even though Salamanda, tea time dance are short-term benefits. But who hears this lone voice

"Who says this country suffers unemployment. See the number of girls just out of college. Lucky ones are already working and the boys.' Don't ask me if they don't want to work.

"They say women are good cashiers. But I have known of this other girl and that other woman both of whom have acquired sticky fingers and a rat-like speed and precision. But the thief is one caught like we know what wrong a politician or Minister has done only when he is out of office.

"Foreign bodies have invaded my system and the poisoned blood flow is slow. If Christmit meets me, I will marry the next round of mass wedding so I can stop fighting the girl who deserted me.

"I dreamt that someone had slapped me, but he was more powerful and my reaction was only to shout. But I was chewing something too much flup in my mouth even to swallow all. So he slapped me again and I could not talk or shout because when your mouth is full you cannot talk.

"The flirting woman who is Finance Minister is checked by the minion and cowed husband. This of course is not true."

iii) "WEDNESDAY AUGUST 21, SALAMANDER PEPER SOUP FOR KUMBA"

"Well, it was humanly impossible to be with you yesterday. I wonder if you would guess what happened to me or where I was. You sabi say nobi all thing dem di talk.

"Any way, I went to this economic place for capital and rain be plenty sotee I wade waist deep in water in order to reach my friend's house.

"In spite of salary increases plenty people dem nobi go for work because water plenty. Most residential areas were flooded and go for work man must pull irosis eoroot.

"Rain di bring bad bisnec a tycoon told we as if they do not want the rain. My army (typical) say bisnec bad for rain time ~ people nobi falla we for rain time.

"I left Diwara for Kumba. You know this thing called 'room charge'. Well some assistant hotel they were asked room charge and the next thing the man knew he was standing in the dock. "Of all the institutions, I raised my cap to the courts. They alone in spite of everything are checking our excesses. The massa been free the case.

"I did drink salamander pepper soup' a Kumba beauty told me. This is a new type of pepper soup with cow foot for Kumba. Also new drink whe dem mix one bottle gini with one bottle gol haf take espe boxam there all this I see for Kumba na better kontri."

iv) "AUGUST 23, 1974: RAIN NA BAD TIME"

"The season when excuses are valid na for rain time. 'You no see rain' is always the valid excuse. So I had a

Chapter Fifteen: Ako-Aya and Misleading Titles

date and I been give fifty for pay taxi sep - it rained and I waited. I saw her in the morning and was furious - you nobi see plenty rain.

"I went to this power house to get my hard-earned money and I was told big man no cam work because of rain.

"My friend goes out a lot during the dry season - one ca understand but what the wife could not understand is why he must go out for this rain time for net. Sometimes he sleeps out because 'rain been lock me.'

"So Madam too been comot when massa been dey up side. They must in the same hotel and this is where I must stop. As to what happened your guess is as good as mine.

"This wharf has given this people who draw plans plenty work.

"Plots in the whole area have been taken up. So I tried going there make myself I get some ground 'massa Ako, this nobi place whe people lake you de buy ground.' Some ground about ten different people dong buyam.

"And yet everyday we cry say money no dey money boku for this contry only say nobi people leke me dem getam.

"You know when nursing started in Nigeria and the early nurses were being trained in Britain, they the Britons were surprised to see males training as nurses. Nurse work na work for woman. Therefore I should have been happier if na woman nurse been rape some boy and not vice-versa. "Perhaps man nurse dew fit go for green revolution while part of my army take them place for hospital."

v)   "APRIL 5, 1974: WANTED - A WIFE"

"Well readers, as I had earlier said, the year 1974 has come with several things. Today I am bringing you a letter written by a desperate celebrated young bachelor.

"Now the letter reads.

"'Dear Mr. Ako Aya,
"'Kindly permit me a space to make a pertinent appeal in your widely read column. I am a young man - one quarter of a century old with no physical deformities. I hold a Bachelor of Arts degree obtained outside Cameroon from one of the most recognised Universities in the world. I live and work in Victoria in one of the big offices where I have a self-contained house and a smart car.

"'I want a beautiful girl for a wife who must have the following qualities;

"'(1) She must be between 20 and 23 years old.
(2) She must have a good pair of legs and a fair complexion.
(3) She must not be less than 5 ft 9 ins or 1.75 metres tall.
(4) Must have at least 4 papers in the General Certificate of Education of which English, and- -Home Economics must be among. Those with higher qualifications will be at advantage.
(5) She must be a virgin- with firm headlamps (breasts).
(6) And she must be prepared to pay the bridegroom's price of 75.000 francs to my father.

"'All interested ladies who deem themselves qualified should send the following :-"'(1) Recent full-size photograph.
(2) Letter of option affixed with 250 fiscal stamp.
(3) Certified true copies of academic qualifications.

Chapter Fifteen: Ako-Aya and Misleading Titles

(4) Birth certificate or birth declaration obtained ONLY from the High Court.
(5) A 50 frs. stamped self addressed envelope.

"'Those who hold a Beauty Queen certificate or have evidence of having participated in a Beauty Contest will be on advantage. All correspondence will be treated in very strict confidence and should be addressed:
CIO The Editor, Cameroon Outlook,
P.O. Box 124,
Victoria, Fako Division,
South West Province.

OR

Through Mr. Thomas AKO-AYA, Provincial Delegate of the Royal,
Army of Unmarried Women,
075 Church Street,
VICTORIA."

vi)   "FRIYDAY APRIL 19, 1974: WOMAN APPLY FOR MAN

"'It was with great pleasure that I read your letter addressed through Mr. Ako-Aya as I am The Very Girl You are Looking For. My photograph speaks for itself. Apart from your other requirements which I found very which I am prepared to give physical evidence when the time comes you will agree that I have a beautiful mouth a sense of humour, laughing eyes and very special earrings.

"'I have a first class honours degree in Gold Hard consumption and can sometimes be found in a well known S.W. Cameroon pub late at night. However I cannot remember ever seeing you there (judging from your self description), but then I didn't look under all the tables.

"'One problem, I have no money and only have a few francs to show for my nightly endeavours. Yes I work night-shift in a very popular Bar where the beer is cheap.

"'I think it best if you encourage me further. 20.000 frs CFA will do and then I will send you a picture of my other attributes.

"'Hoping we come to an amicable understanding. Yours in advance; (picture was affixed.) Virginia EDLAMP.'
"The above letter from Virginia Edlamp is in response to our bachelor friend looking for a wife."

Chapter Sixteen

Ako-Aya and Christmas

Ako-Aya never failed to wish his readers a 'Happy Christmas.' And it was in such articles that he articulated on the various financial problems which family members have to face up to. This is moreso because gifts have to be bought. Of course, like he rightly pointed out, January is often a difficult month for many, as all that had been saved was used up for Christmas entertainments. He wrote:

i) "FRIDAY JAN. 1, 1971; HAPPY1! HAPPY!"

"Christmas found me on the mail van bound for the North. I wanted to get away from it all, what with the pretentious greetings of 'Merry Xmas.' Even my enemy came to shake hands with me on this day and this woman who drinks twenty gallons of water everyday to shake her unquenchable thirst was wishing me happy, happy, several days before 25th.

"I got to the North at this place of the big river feeling dusty. Two thousand francs changed hands with the driver for seating at the back. I didn't blame him, he had a right to enjoy Xmas at my expense.

"There was a fund-raising dance organized by a football club. I went to the dance first to sea why dances are staged in this place only on Friday and to look at the girls. I had no explanation to my enquiry but had a good eyeful of the girls - fat, small, tall, long, short tumbu and all in all.

"I paid 200 francs to get into this dance not so much for the sake of the dance than to help a football club - suddenly a something officer came with a big agbada as if he had just had an Alhajirate from Mecca University. He glided passed the gates without so much as directing his eyes to where the tickets are sold. The clerk at the gate sent him a small note asking for donations and the man rose to his full height and refused to pay any donations. 'Don't you know I am privileged and I have immunity even up to not paying donations.' He further threatened the clerk with a sack-such naked display of power. "I know that even the Big VIPS donate to worthy causes but not his lesser official. Veil, was it not happy happy I left that hall and town a changed man, and destroyed all the greeting cards sent to me. There is none who really wishes the other a Merry Xmas and Happy New Year. I have been asked by the Editor of this paper to compile my 1970 writings into book form. I intend to sell the book for 100 francs. "Next issue - my New Year Resolution."

ii) <u>"FRIDAY DEC. 3, 1971: KAM FOR OFFICE"</u>

"I have been thinking of leaving this work and being a servant of the people who pay tax. Think of the money and authority, for example you can ask anybody to 'Kam for your office and he will be "shaking" to come.

"So I went to borrow some money from one of my big friends, 'Look Thomas' he said 'I don't have a mite, I'm living on 0.0.' but he took the telephone and rang the chairman 'Masse i bad, we no fit hold meeting?' he then asked we to come back in two days and after that he gave me the money 'part of my allowance' he told me gladly. "They get their pay, they get duty salaries, and they get ten thousand francs each day when they attend meetings and of course it must take several meetings to reach a decision.

Chapter Sixteen: Ako-Aya and Christmas

"Then one of these men saw a beautiful girl selling in a shop in Tiko. But as Tiko has very few girls they all have their 'permanent people.' This servant of the people made advances but they were repulsed by the women.

"As a servant, he merely sent a note demanding her presence and she came all the way from Tiko to Victoria. 'I wan show you se I get power, you go sleep here today.' But the girl refused and returned. You may think they are your servants because your taxes pay them, but make no mistake about it, they are your masters and are riding rough-shod over you.

"The fights are on the increase my massa nobi buy me something for Christmas. Homes are breaking, friends are separating and the cry is for money. Even the Kumba so-so stand wants money to go to Oku. Several people in fact are planning a trip to Oku this month. "Bye till next issue."

iii)   "FRIDAY JAN. 17, 1972: MONEY DON FINISH"

"First of all I must apologise to all my fans for the long silence. It is none of my doing, nor of the newspaper itself but of the printers who went on a holiday. You know the effect of this Xmas and New Year.

"So after thanking my creator for permitting not only I but my many friends and enemies to see this big New Year I went to this other Church at least to thank my Creator a second time. I stood open mouthed as a big quarrel ensured in Church with this society and that crossing words. 'My house is the house of prayer but you have turned it into a house of thieves.'

"I shudder and fear for myself to write about many things. What of the Doctors' fight in Buea, and of course you know this little can be misleading as even a medicine man is a Native Doctor. What of the fights in Tiko, the 'Na so I fine' of Victoria what of this dance where 'dem take we money and drive we se we no get suit.' But of course Luncheon date, its drowsy voice producer and high pitched baby voiced co-producer and their attach on West Cameroon papers. Maybe like that medium which sings Vietnam and Israel every day these papers at least say something of Bamenda and Ndian. But as I say, I fear for myself to write about some of these things.

"I was supposed to write about money dong finish.' Truly it is finished - debts remained unpaid and the hotel bills and school fees once paid by post-dated cheques. The one that beats all was the one issued by car owner N° W 2 of Buea for staying in a Kumba hotel. He issued a post-dated cheque for 2-1-73. Principals of schools are no longer accepting these P.d.c.'s one of them waves a sheath of cheques at me. 'How many of these will go through, but had I not warned before Xmas?

"Even food is hard to be eaten these days in certain houses. But let the 25th come and most of our ills will be cured."

Chapter Seventeen

Ako-Aya and the Fall of the City of Victoria

Ako-Aya, like many 'Victorians' saw Victoria rise and fall. In one of his articles, 'Christmit Weekend for Fitolia', he lamented the decline and hotly criticised the government for neglecting the natural seaport in Victoria.
He wrote:

> "WEDNESDAY DEC. 5, 1973:
> CHRISTMIT WEEK-END FOR FITOLIA"
>
> "This week-end I spent it in Va. after clear six months of spending weekends out of this municipality,
> "I tell you I enjoy the job I do always on the move, with a detachment of my army sprayed all over the places I visit.
>
> "Well, you know my favourite town is Kumba with its teaming population, its coffee and cocoa now being sun-dried and oh - its women - women who now specialise in 'gin with he falla back' or the new craze of whisky/becks.
>
> "Well, I spent what I thought would end up a quiet week end in this ghost town with its two universities the comprehension one and now this library I hear is a new university brought home.
> "Whom or where did I not visit. I visited my friend the Mayor with his ever smiling wife
> 'where have you been' they asked together in unison.
>
> "However, I am trying this whisky/becks combination and they gave me.

"I visited a detachment of my army along Church Street and noticed that the Bororos of the No where province are enlisting in great quantities.

"I spoke to my 'behind I,C.C. sergeant N° M.7924/68 and she reported all was quiet.

"I spoke to another sergeant N° L.385/73 and she reported that she was unable to cope with the worries of Teroris in At and Mira hotels. She had already sent word for more troops.

"Believe me, if I was not learning to be a priest by correspondence course, perhaps I should have invoked the gods of Oku for punishment.

"The trade in Human beings that goes on in the evenings between these teroris and my army staggers the imagination.

"I am only glad that my brothers of the Taxi David have a good cut from this trade because after 7 the fare to these hotels is 150.

"I went to films as usual and to the Bell. Its becoming a good place to spend week-ends now - good soft music, cool drinks and the soya. I am not going to tell you who took me to the Bell or who or what, I danced with. Anyway, I met a friend of mine from Yawinde. He told me of his purse stolen from the train, containing 90.000 francs and how the computer had sent his pay to Fort Fureau to a messenger who bears the same name as him while the messenger's pay was sent to him he a whole chief of ...

"Anyway, I ended up by 'trossing' all the drinks for him and he gave me a P.D. cheque on an obscure bank in Bertoua.

Chapter Seventeen: Ako-Aya and the Fall of the City of Victoria

"I spent part of the week-end in Tiko however for this titam dance at the El-Port hotel. This titam dance in Tiko is not a jokish affair.

"Some Massa and Madam came with their 8 1/2 children. In Victoria titam is for young people but not Tiko.

"Most of the girls at this dance came from my army in Tiko. Perhaps Tiko should learn to send army officers to the fishing ports and recruit young army officers for the town.

"Anyway, Titam in Tiko is a grand affair. Try and attend some Sunday, you will surely meet friends from Buea, Victoria and Douala.

"Anyway this Victoria affair when they say 'business dong fall my grandmother bobi', something has to be done about it. They say in good English which I equally know 'the strength of a chain is its weakest link.'

"Personally, I am tired of words and speeches.
I like to see the Refinery up and the wharf - nobody hears about it again even the palms CDC were to fell for the land around the wharf are still being harvested.

"Victoria is a deep sea-port, an asset which most African land locked areas would give their lives to get. Let us make use of it instead of wasting money dredging the undredgable.
I pause hoping this town will prosper like when Alfred Saker founded it or when the Germans transferee/ the whole Headquarters of Cameroon to Buea.

"Happy Christmit."

The people truly respected and admired this journalist. And this because he always had their interest at heart. Who would have thought that it would not be regarded as subversive informing the government that it was misdirec-ting the tax-payers' money by spending it in dredging the Douala Port when Victoria housed a naturally deep sea port. Ako-Aya knew the implications but this did not disturb him for he was bent on a cause. You would come to see in the later part of this book that, the wharf and the oil refinery in Victoria became Ako-Aya's life-long ambition -he wanted to see them take off.

The city was hit harder when in November 1972 property worth about 300 million francs was consumed by a big fire. In the articles which follow, Ako-Aya aptly described the hard decline in the economy of Victoria from 1972. It was so bad that he termed it a 'Ghost Town.' In a bid to vivify this once prosperous city, he occasionally brought out a few latent points that still made Victoria great.

He wrote:

i) "WEDNESDAY JUNE 1972: VICTORIA LIFE"

"When last I wrote about Kumba, it was not meant to paint a glorious picture of the place but to bring you the human side of some every day affairs in that gay metropolis. Today the next town to take the floor is this sea-side town - Victoria. Quite a place in those days with banana boats calling 7 days a week, today ships take their time before they come to Victoria. "It is a good place to come from, its Victoria with its magnificent building at the sea front and its pot holes and dirty roads. Perhaps Victoria excels in women employment than any town in the state with its giant Corporations and multiplicity of Banks. Here the problem lies.

"To get married to a Victoria girl you must promise to pay half a monthly salary to her personal account and it is not your business how she spends it. If it is only 'girl-friend business' you know then you must place her on a monthly allowance of at least 10.000 francs. No wonder all of them are still 'Miss' at the ages of 50. No wonder too, every body is afraid of these sharks and they must travel out of this town to satisfy themselves, money or no money. No wonder we lost most of them to 'Okrika merchant and to tycoons from the Ease'

"Another menace is the Victoria land-lord with a teaming population with business then becoming a room - 'bock' is 2.500 francs. Nearby Tiko and Kumba offer half the rents and most women are moving. Not only women are moving but Nigeria people dem di go because business ojoronjo.'

"Everybody says 'business i bad' and everybody hopes the wharf will improve everything. If a wharf would improve it, why don't we build a wharf here instead of wasting time because I hear it said that by the time we reach 2058 that is when the town will be celebrating its 200th year it may no longer be there.

"But come to Victoria at night and you will think it is a heaven on earth. There is no money they say, yet there are more pubs than schools.

"'Massa no bi mimbo this.'
"Then there is this new 'Township Taxi ' now plying our streets. The other day I was going to see my wife in 'Buta' and I entered one of these taxis. By the time we reached there the seats being so old had torn my 'troser nyi las' and she had to bring a loin cloth to tie in order to walk from the public to her house.

"This is Victoria founded by Alfred Saker in 1858 and named after the English Queen: This is Victoria in 1972.

"I wrote last about Victoria girls how untrust-worthy they are; I did not get in mind that boys should also 'kiaful' for their friends. 'One is sometimes promoted because of hard work; but this friend working with one of this money houses up half-mile because a junior staff who happened to be his friend was doubly promoted instead of him praying to his Allah for his own turn of promotion, resorted to 'Munuku' so that his friend may end up in the land of see-roe-no more. His sister was also used in the plot. His boss was called upon to intervenes but who knows the ways of these bank people and of medicine men. Who does not know what hatred can do and this dying woman who asked her husband for a blue-lace garment."

ii) <u>FRIDAY NOV. 17, 1972: I NO BI TALK?"</u>

"When two years ago I wrote in this column that Mr. Fusi of Lagos then on leave should remain and start the nucleus of a fire brigade service, of course, I was told to shut my big mouth and the usual word of 'subversive' was labelled on me.

"So I went to this great fire of London, I beg your pardon great fire of Victoria. It appeared all the people 'dem dey for cinema as nobody did a thing.' Then tif people too wan try for work' and again of course the people provided another meeting place for lovers.

"As there was no water people try trowe Gol haf for loss fire but Gol haf na for belle nobi for loss fire.

"Anyway, I am not going to write about this fire any more. I am going to write how I spent fifteen day in Tiko note that I have not used any plural in the day. Fifteen day is when we for shidishi de take 'small pay.' The amount ranges from 500 frs. to 2,000 francs.

Chapter Seventeen: Ako-Aya and the Fall of the City of Victoria

"First I went to this Hotel without an airport. A big Hall, very good music but sabit dem plenty pass customer.

"From here we vent though the town which is taking on a new look. I peeped into Domino and met a lovely woman and asked her for a dance (you no sabi say my man na big man for Banana.' I wondered what a big banana man's wife should be doing single at a dancing joint around mid-night. "The girls no longer go to hotels and so the big men leave their cars far away and walk to where the girls live, normally dark, filthy spots.

"The fast life in Tiko is slowing down because 'woman dem no dey.' When Calabar women were buying halfpenny fat in order to be fat, we were laughing at them. These days na only white-man like 'small woman'. Most people like'em fat what we call rains-seas woman. So the girls buy custards food in order to have this plummy look. No wonder Bird's Custard dong dear, and I couldn't get a tin for my lovely daughter. I heard this at break-fast table yesterday.
Can I sign off now?"

iii) <u>"FEBRUARY 4, 1976: NA BLOCKADE DE REIGN NOW</u>

"The times are really changing very adversely . Once one thought things can hardly be tight for business men and the loose girls on whom they lavish their money. But alas, things are different.

"These days everybody is turning to 'blockade.' And so I met a bevy of girls quarrelling over a blockade meal.

"'When una dey pass for road una dey high, weti you de fight for' one of them shot at the other. "'You no sabi say me I try self. Some girls dem dey here wey no fit even chop blockade for their house', she replied.

"She was very near the truth. Times are hard these days especially after the Xmas season. "Auditors would discover wonders if they check the books of cashiers now because the privately borrowed funds for Xmas are yet to be met up."

iv) <u>"FRIDAY OCT. 29,</u> 1973: VICTORIA DON FLOP"

"For first day for November for this year 'teroris' will be arriving Victoria on their usual fortnight stay.

"The population of Victoria is going to double itself as women from all over Cameroon are already taking up rooms in the hotels and some renting seasonal houses.

"Some of these teroris come here in order to follow the sun, others come because Cameroon woman dem sabi make that thing well because the African women's sex powess is higher than their European counterparts.

"The homosexual come here because some of the youth are poor and will not mind too much if their bodies are misused for seka money. However the women coming here from Douala and environs have a high purchasing power and dem go buy plenty thing from our shops.
"Mark you do not forget that Grande Camarade been talk say make Akwara finish and people caught will be dealt with the law. Even land lords who give their houses on rents to prostitutes dem commit offence."

"BLACK OUT ...
"Lest I forget, this is the letter got from a reader in Kumba.

"'Dear Mr. Thomas Ako-Aya,
"'My problem is a love one. I have a girl who works in the education department here in Kumba. She is such a

Chapter Seventeen: Ako-Aya and the Fall of the City of Victoria

devout Catholic that I can only have sex with her only after she has taken a bit of alcohol. She needs about four bottles of big Guinness to make her feel gay. My monthly salary is not adequate and so its only at month end that I can afford to buy 4 large Guinness at one sitting which means I can only have sex with her once a month.

"However I would want to have sex with her general times but for any handicap.
"So sir, I hear you are too knowing, can you or your readers tell we what I should do?
"ERNEST AKAMA KUMBA"

"Well readers, can you help our friend Ernest. I don't know what is becoming of the world. Everything seems to be going the other way round.

"When I was an infant theft was only associated with males. But not so these days. Girls are taking over like mad.

"Pick-pocketing, shop lifting, burgling, lies telling, swindling, everything, the girls are in. And so this society girl was picked yesterday for shop lifting. Poor thing. The pant costs only 250 francs but there she was standing in the midst of the crowd."

v)   "<u>WEDNESDAY NOV. 14, 1973:</u>
        <u>TOR1S DONG COME</u>"

"Once again this ghost town is springing back into life. We have teroris from the Continent and now we have teroris from Douala. Houses along church street are fully blocked and for land-lord 'this Christmit go better small.'

"Kumba is becoming such a big city that it is becoming as full of lies as Douala.

"This is how I hot-footed it to Kumba the other day when I heard my friend was dead. I reached Kumba and made straight for the grave-yard.

"I saw my friend, but, he was not dead, he had gone into hiding because of debts. He gave out the story that he was dead. I reached his house and one of his creditors came to see if he was really dead, he fell down crying 'my money - o, My money o.'

"Well so is life. That is why these days in this ghost town I drink in off-licences. Try going into proper drinking places and this my army from Douala are quarrelling among themselves.

"Some people are very kind like my friend I met in Kumba. Since his son came from mid-term from college he has not returned and yet he is sponsoring his gf's son in college.

"You know the other day he had to go on tour like myself to Pamda and then he made arrangements with a girl teaching in Victoria and another working in Tiko Council all to meet him at the Lingway.

"But he got to Pamda and these girls got to Pamda and he found out that he had actually carried coal to Newcastle. He woke me up at night to give me one of the girls from the coast but like him I found the Pamda girls a better morsel and turned his offer down.

"See you on Friday."

Chapter Seventeen: Ako-Aya and the Fall of the City of Victoria

vi)   "DECEMBER 17, 1976:
            GHOST TOWN DONG WAKE-UP"

"Our Ghost town is up. All parts and things that make up Victoria are bursting at the seems. Take a simple thing like land - all the hills and valleys and swamps are in the process of being all taken.

"There is also an influx of my troops believe me this one dem fine pass mark; But I sat on the balcony to hear names being read and no hear my own name. Na weti me I do?

"For this eight people, five for comot for Va even massa way get chair for comot - Va. After all we have been living in the ghost town.
"Proper me self or even you whe di read this my book if dem give you chop for month you no go chop 'am?

"They say Christmit time dong reach. During this time there is only one thing you must do - call a halt with G.F. 's. Remember second term fees and also your children must enjoy Xmas. The best time for reconciliation is after the New Year.

"When you travel to Kumba or Mamfe and somebody offers you a drink make sure the drinks are paid for first before you drink dem otherwise you will end up by paying for them.

"Paul did it to me at Azi Motel in Kumba while Robinson did the same thing to me a Besong-Abang. Can a doctor in-charge of a hospital take up as a tutor in a take up part-time of appointment as a tutor in a college? or an MP also take up an appointment as the pastor of a Presbyterian church.

"I tell you none of us is satisfied with the salaries we earn. We are always looking for additions. This is one way things are and will be."

Chapter Eighteen

Ako-Aya and Fraud in the Bota Wharf

It has been argued that the fall of the city of Victor! was caused by the departure of the foreigners who perpetrated the famous fraud in the Bota wharf. The result was that, no second hand clothes were imported, while prostitutes understandably condemned the investigations. D fact, they claimed that it was a flagrant demonstration d jealousy on the part of those who investigated the fraud This argument of jealousy did not stop Ako-Aya from telling us how these girls suffered when the wharf frauds left Victoria. In fact, he did not miss the opportunity to express his total disgust for this fraudulent behaviour by foreign business men.

He wrote:

i) "WEDNESDAY JANUARY 13, 1971: ASHIYA"

"When I was young and used to steal, my old father told me 'many day for tif man and one day for man wey i get farm.' So, how else could I take this than when I went over the week-end to visit ay contri girl. Go quick my boy di cam' she told me. The 'boy' turned out to be one of these bald-headed people with very big cars. He immediately passed her ten thousand francs CFA for 'market money.'

"So as my father said 'many day for tif man ...' I use to wonder how somebody can give a girl ten thousand francs every market day, and such days are thrice a week. I used to wonder how a man can buy a frigedaire for a girl, build her a block house, and do all sort of things. I know I am ugly, but how many girls ever fought on my behalf - no they must fight for these rich people who are able to do these things for them. But did they know where the money was coming from -and how many of these girls are involved in Victoria - a legion. These female bank clerks in all the banks, these PWD clerks and Highway 'Robbers.' Some of these very many girls working in our Bookshops, Government and Corporation offices with their 'long long sanjas' all sat weeping because their tycoons had been arrested. What have these wen done, this country they don't like men who progress'.

"Yes, according to these girls even though the Government of the Federal Republic of Cameroon has been cheated to the tune of a hundred milliard for several years, it does not matter as long as they get five thousand francs every market day. What matters to them if the Government is cheated and over five thousand teachers cannot be paid. What matters if Government cannot maintain existing roads, if there were no vehicles plying from Victoria to Kumba to Bamenda. All that matters is if the tycoons can buy them sanjas to cover their gutted feet.

"But as far as an enemy to my country is an enemy to me I say Ashiya to all these girls who have been crying themselves hoarse over the week-end. Well all day for tif man but one day and that day is today massa wey i get farm. Ashiya~eh."

ii)   "<u>JANUARY 20, 1971: NA JEALOUSIE</u>"

While everybody has been showing some concern on the amount of money that has eluded us, money that rightly belongs to you I met two very pretty girls who thought differently. 'Una di jealouse them' one of them told me. The one, a dark-slimmed beauty with dual nationality, the other a former beauty queen from the land where coffee bangs and fens.

Chapter Eighteen: Ako-Aya and Fraud in the Bota Wharf

"Well they said, we were lazy people, unable to work as hard as our brothers, the other side of cross-river. They said we 'tight hand' and even if we have money we could not give anybody even one franc.

"But they say one of them has 'medicine pot' in her room which when stirred while calling somebody's name, the man must give her money. So, as they say she is very wealthy, with several plots of land and in her house there are several fridges and gas-cookers, as for the carpet you could sleep rather than walk on it. "I have been thinking much of a medicine pot, all the power it holds when these girls, their conversation continued 'as for that Ako-Aya he wowo pas medicine pot' they both agreed.

"I thought a medicine pot held so much power, little do I know that it is also wowo.
"I told you about this malaria fever that is eating up my bones. I have never been afraid of death than when I laid a few days ago sick with malaria and almost dying. There was no reason for me to be afraid of death, in fact it would be an easier way for all troubles, the debts and the enemies.

"Then in this traditional moment I met one of the seven angels. Are you a Doctor, he asked because here we have no need for Doctors since no one is sick. He continued to say that there was no need for farmers since everybody had plenty of food, no need for Administrators since everybody was so good, not to talk of Lawyers, who would think of crime in that land. I then told them that I was a journalist - I educate, inform and entertain people, 'Educate, the angel said nobody here needs education but inform and entertain yes we would need your services more and when time was up I would be re-called.

"I woke up from my trance, my fever gone - so of all profession of the world only the services of journalists will be required in heaven. You may argue this if you don't agree."

Iii)   "FEBRUARY 16, 1971:
        <u>DEM JAM STONE</u>"

"The one thing we have to thank the swindlers for is the way they helped our women. Why, merely to plait her hair a girl was given five thousand francs by one of them 'takem tie head.' If you don' t believe this look at the way since the swoop that the girls are 'entering trouble. Take this former beauty queen for instance who works in a very reputable bank and who Kalu gave everything from gas-cooker to false breasts and now that he is away and she is not able to live a life she has been used to, now she hobnobs with car thieves in order to raise more money. If I owned money in the bank I would prevail on the bank Manager to sack 'for conduct not condusive to the furtherance of the good name of the bank' - but this is only my suggestion.

"Take this other woman in Mokeba farms in love with a school teacher who has not been paid for months - had an abariba boy-friend and yet was Mr. Her source of revenue is detained and she cannot even afford money to buy stockfish from the market. So she is alleged to have resorted to stealing. All these crimes by our women were not there when the Abariba people were around, but what can I do about it.

"Take this other long legged girl also in the bank by the way I suggested that the banks, the highways and the obang people should screen the girls they now employ as they damage their good names. Well take this girl, I met her my way back from Oku to look for 'medicine to get another rich man.' She told the medicine man

Chapter Eighteen: Ako-Aya and Fraud in the Bota Wharf

that she use to save all her salary and the men bought drinks and food including goat soya at the Bay for her. She has now bought a pot to manage my life.'

"But what of the other half educated or stark illiterates plus a lot of good looks. They still find an excuse for drinking Beck, Heinekins and Meta Heinekins - 'Dem cook dem water whe Chorola no day inside' - but who of us can afford these drinks. When special people go by special.

"I met Ambollah, one of these half educated ones 'i c who could never pass standard one 'no touch my head, you no bi abariba man'. Well they annoyed me merely for writing what has happened and being true to my fatherland, to them as long as 5.000 frs exchanged hands, the swindlers did nothing wrong.

"Well, it is now likely that I may be given an assistant and will only work on this paper part time. I am now looking for a job and next issue I will tell you how I answered an advertisement to fill a vacant post in these big corporations that litter our country. Don't say I haven't the qualifications, no, I am just unlucky by bearing my names and tribe front which I come is not that which many 'big people' come from. So I lost, the job and who got it?."

iv)   "WEDNESDAY MAY 26, 1971:
          <u>WE eiASSA DEM PONG COME</u>"

"All this happened exactly 7 days ago. The old women asked me 'my pikin this good Ibo people whe bad people hold them for Buea, whose time dem go lef dem' she then told me how she, her child and grand children had been suffering. Leutis sep, we noba pay for 5 months. It was a pitiable sight for girls who had been used to cooking with gas to go back once again to firewood, girls to whom Beck and Heinekens were their favourites now move to Ngangi and girls who had 5.000 to plait their hair now not sure of 500 francs for the market. 'Then it all changed and the order to release them went out - and so they paid their fines and staggered forth looking so lean such that their own mothers could not have known them.

"The news went round and next morning which was a public holiday several of the women friends to these men chartered all the drinks in a pub. "They drank and they sang 'we massa dem dong -come', all we trouble dong finish.' Some said how pikin he milik just finish yesterday and others how just now I go born for senior service Hospital and yet others said how my hair dong chacara for moon today.

"For believe me this happy-go lucky women are very lucky. Just when the swindlers left the tourists came in and just when the Tourists left, the swindlers are back.

"As for the swindlers, now that some of them have paid their fines, I wonder whether they are still swindlers. But I hope they would have learnt a big lesson. Let them stop displaying so much money 'you care for this' should stop and those they begun to build for the women let them call a halt.

"It was this wanton display of money, this 5.000 francs tied round watches that brought them in the lime-light.

"But what of 'those who escaped, will their own women now say 'if them bi day dem for left them too.'

"But this is the way things are."

v)   "FRIDAY JULY 9, 1971:
                        OKRIKA DONG DIE"

"Chineke.' my friend shouted as he was told this morning that a ban had been placed on second hand clothing, what we fondly called 'Okrika.'

"You know this Okrika business used to help some of us - I do not remember me entering a shop to buy a shirt or a coat but all my shirts, ties coats and shoes are Okrika and it is surprising how much they cost.

"500 francs and I am glad as a gentleman and my friend's wife buys all her bras and handbags from this same source. The other day I saw her in church, typically American dressed and all for less than a bottle of beer.

"But what of this double car numbers that repeat themselves, what of my sisters who indirectly are affected by the ban of this trade, will they be given 5 thousand to tie head again and what of the uncompleted?

"Believe me 'I sorry to them.' It has become like the time when the slave trade was stopped – how the slave Millionaires crumbled down like a pack of cards."

Chapter Nineteen

Ako-Aya - A Prophet of his Death

I have always considered some of the articles written by late Obenson in 1976 and 1977 to be more of prophesies. As it had been earlier remarked his main concern later became that of the oil in Victoria. Sadly enough, he had very difficult moments with his health during this period. Small wonder that he took the pains to tell us of his death, which as he rightly prophesied, came before the official inaugu-ration of the oil refinery. Thus on Saturday, July 17th 1976, he wrote:

"I SAW OUR WEALTH DOWN BELOW

"I went up to the mountain top and saw glory, I might not even reach there with you... Martin Luther some time made this statement in America. He was really a Messiah in the Twentieth century "But me Mr. Ako-Aya Thomas, commander of the poor say I saw the glory of tomorrow now fellow country men, I might not be with you when those that be make the final say. The father gave it to us for us all.

"Then I cam to Douala for inside there na luck mup. Them tell me say that whiteman who was sent away in the Douala oys company is back again. I thought that foreigners who come into our country with bad intents, once sent out must never be allowed to enter the country. The case of this oya guy puzzles me.

"I have seen our wealth down below, I might not be around by the time it is around but no matter where it is brought out all the money for it is put into the national money pot."

And in more forceful language he wrote again in 1977:

"I DE FEAR DIE"

"The recent deaths have sent shrills through my spine. You know when someone far away from you dies it hardly means a thing to you but when death crawls right into your house or office you just begin to think the next victim would be you.

"And so I have been having nightmares all these days. I saw myself being dressed and stayed quiet throughout the process but when the coffin arrived, it dawned on me that it was really the end of me and I started yelling and took to my heels. But instead for the people for glad say I dong wake up, they chased me, caught me and were about to force me into the coffin. I was struggling with the people when I woke up. I was soaked in sweat.

"Day before that I dreamt that I was electricuted by an electric line cut by myself.
'But one dream which does not worry me much is the one I had last Sunday. I saw myself being forcefully dressed in white shorts and short-sleeved shirts after which the men began shaving me. You can guess what they wanted to do to me. However, if that is what was in their minds then I can readily say I am used to such things.

"I shoulder to write about many things these days. I even fear to write about this President of this club with the name of a river. I would not say that he was the prime mover behind the closure of an off-licence near their club because he alleges it was disturbing their market but today yi sep-sep dong open yi own uplasin for yi house. And the house is nearer the club than the closed off-licence was. But that is our way of life.

Chapter Nineteen: Ako-Aya - A Prophet of his Death

"This greed for money will send people to extremes these days. Even my army too has begun devising new ways of exploiting us.

"If you go to a harlot's house these days, make sure she does not have a female child. Even if the child is one year old, take your time. Also don't allow her leave you in the house and pretend she is going to urinate. If you do, she will come back and raise an alarm alleging she met you trying to defile her child. And since they always congregate together, all of them would come out and support her. That would black-mail and say if you don't pay hush money, they would take you to the law officers. So take your time.

"So much has been said about bribery, so much has been written against it, even those who take it most condemn it and in spite of all this con-demnation, the thing goes on with unabated fury.

"By bribery and its twin brother corruption, I do not mean the two hong whe messenger di take for road when one does not carry his tax ticket. I do not mean the two hong makara parti whe droba di give we friend for road for tell them ashia for mosquito whe di bite them but I mean the huge sky-scraper amounts, goods and chattels in the name of happy Christmas and New Year.

"So I did not attend this maret of the year. I hear say bride price na un million. "Can I get tired about this thing they call Christmit. To me it is a day we celebrate the birth of a child called Jesus. Jesus is the son of God and he came into this earth to redeem us from sin.

"At least this much I have learnt from my pastor at the Baptist Church. But the whole celebration has been commercialised to the extent that we lose the sight of the fact that it is a child's birthday we are celebrating.

"This time the breweries are working 25 hours a day in order to provide drinks for Christmit, traders have started receiving their orders for the Xmas and fowls, goats, cows and pigs for cry for their last for Xmas.

"Now for our women its the time for billing the men. Market dem di spoil, girl friend dem di run, boy friend dem di hide all this for seka Xmas. This is the time you can give blife to your boss with an eye on the next promotion. This is when goats and yams di pass for Yawinde for Happy Xmas.

"But in all we do, let us not forget say na birthday for God he pikin we de celebrate.
"I had often wondered what the fuse is all about concerning this famla thing until I met this hotel tycoon in our business bubbling Bafoussam the other day doing what I can hardly find a term to describe.

"Should I continue with that story or tell you about this corruption bill? I will rather shelve both for now and talk about the newly painted Bafoussam void of dilapidated buildings and dust bins."

Chapter Twenty

Ako-Aya's Last Few Months on Earth

Although this great journalist must have had nightmares of his death in 1975 and 1977, he still was not discouraged writing on. Indeed, his job was not in any way jeopardised. Unfortunately, we could not read much of his works in 1979, that being the year when he died. As early as January of this same unforgettable year, 1979, he came out with a series of articles which he called FOOLISH DREAMS; were they really nightmarish dreams of his bad health, thus his decision to write of his death; or they were merely dreams of how he would have wished Victoria in particular and Cameroon in general to look like. These are the few articles he wrote during his last few months:

"WEDNESDAY JANUARY 3, 1979:
MY FOOLISH DREAMS AGAIN"

"Believe me a New Year is here now, the nights have become a time of torment and torture for me. , These days I even fear as night conies. You will see me walking to the pubs first to wear-off most ., of the night but as it is even dangerous to walk at night because you may be mistaken for an armed robber and you can easily spend the night sleeping on a soft cement floor with your hands for a pillow;

"So take the other night for instance, I was torn between going out for a drink or being caught up when I decided to stay home and read. The first book that came my way was one on Adolf Hitler, straight-away the dreams came on. Hitler became our big man and my tribe became the Jews.

"We were bound hand and foot and my lovely daughter and I were to be thrown into the gas chambers at once.

As soon as they got hold of us I shouted, sweat pouring all over my body. My partner has since threatened me with a divorce suit for generally shouting and disturbing her at night during sleep and for cruelty because of this.

"So this is it you know what happens to me when I pub walk and then when I sleep and dream. Divorce awaits me, as if most women are not generally disturbed at night by men-folk. Some by snoring so loud, others by other means.
The night I was reading Dr. Fonlon's exposition on Universities. Straight-away dreams took on again. I saw a University centre in Buea - good building, professors with seven doctorate degrees each and smart looking under graduates carrying very many books under their armpits.
'In the dream, I .saw an under-graduate and a friend of mine was the head of an agitation group that thought Buea was not a good site for the university. My friend comes from one of the divisions whose names start with an- 'M' and he thought his division was more appropriate to site the varsity. In this assistance, I disagreed with my friend. The disagreement led to a quarrel and then to a fight. We fought and fought, I was bleeding all over then he jumped on my neck, I gasped for a breath but I never said 'I beg.' Then my friend turned into a magician and ordered the university, its buildings. Professors and all the students to transport itself to this 'M' Division,

"I also became a magician and then ordered it back to Buea. I suddenly woke up. The one I had last night appears so real that up till now I fear to narrate it. But I must continue to narrate my dreams and I will bring you this one next time.

Chapter Twenty: Ako-Aya's Last Few Months on Earth

"MY NEW YEAR RESOLUTIONS

"At midnight on 1st January 1979, I suddenly found myself one year older and nearer the grave than last year. In spite of this people say we should be happy over the New Year - who am I to say No, especially as I have had to rest for three days.

"But believe me, Christmas dong chop New Year. The festivities I saw during Xmas are all gone and the New Year has started with the wrong foot - it looks gloomy. Next week we are going to be called upon to pay school fees, buy uniforms and books. Do not ask me where money is going to come from because I had warned you.

"THIS YEAR

"I am going to continue to thank that Being they call God who has preserved me for all these years. When I see the suffering of others to my present state, I have every reason to thank Him.

"THIS YEAR

"I have learnt that no human organisation can be perfect and so I do not expect perfection in this sole political party in my country. However, I am going to support it financially and morally. But I do not envisage any elections this year 1979 so should there be any I'll want to sing like Prince Nico say this na my choice.

"This year I am not going to ask or take any bribes. I am not going to cheat my employer and misuse his money. I am going to try and be kind to my fellow men and not beat them up or give them muddy water to drink.

"WEDNESDAY JAN. 7, 1979: FOR DANCE HALL"

"The other day I was present at a dance to jubilate the successful taking over of a hotel formerly owned by a Lawyer but now by a Banker. Do not ask me how or why a banker should become a hotelier. All I know is that the race to get rich is so in-born in some of us that we forego all decency.

"Have you heard of this personal manager who combines produce buying with many of his other business. What of this our important engineer for gofmen who has taken to selling coffins. I thought I heard that our supposed servants yet in reality our masters should not engage in biz. Believe me I wonder whether such orders are merely to grace our books or are meant to be kept. Take the administrative reforms for example, the very next day even as an underlining I was being promoted over the heads of older and more qualified people.

"The reason is my wife. You see you can and should no more marry for love if you want any progress in your work place.

"You should marry jal for any bigman nyi country, so that some person can put in a good word of you. This is why second wives are coming in.

"Well, I have off the point as I was telling you earlier of this dance I attended. I noticed one thing that in spite of the music, everybody was dancing his own way, and was the hall not packed full and didn't everybody enjoy himself? "But I tell you some white men are spoiling our dance - they want us to be enemies into our-selves; can you tell me why you should give the meat meant for your children to dogs? Can you tell me why a man should lose employment."

Chapter Twenty: Ako-Aya's Last Few Months on Earth

"TUESDAY JAN. 16, 1979: HOW FOR DASH FOR BONNE ANNEE

"Just after New Year I visited Diwala to buy a few things for .my children who were going back to school. I entered one of the shops and with the list in my hand I thought the shopkeeper will welcome me gladly; on the contrary he was asking me 'weti' you keep me for bonne Annee?

"You may be surprised to learn that he refused to sell most of the things to me saying they were out of stock all because I did not give dash for New Year. I pointed this out to him that he was losing customers and he said he did not care of his pay at fin de mois.

"This is the sort of feast that pervades the bread we are trying to bake. I went to an Indian shop and this time the boss himself served me with a smile. From the shop I moved to this new seventeen storeyed building which is the headquarters of this New Produce Marketing Board.
The building which we the farmers of this country have helped to build, I now understand why the HQ. of this Board could not have been in Victoria, it would have been the only the such without any such buildings to compete with.

"I have seen farmers' houses in Foussam Melam Mbongang and the real producers do not have such smartly furnished houses as the people who only sell. Perhaps since all persons engaged in such flashy furnished house make dem give farmers more chemical for fight back - pod and give we plenty money for cocoa so that we too can have money and finish our houses. This reminds me of the story of the giraffe and the ant which has made the giraffe to have long neck.

NA WHO SELL

"When I look at the things that people do, things that people say I wonder. And when I tell you what people do in the dark corners of this so-so tanap town - you will ask big man to award me the highest honour ever bestowed on a single Cameroonian. Many years ago my honest mother told me how thieves would write you a letter saying they were coming to your house. In the stead of waiting for them to come and make their choice of your property, you were advised to put goods for them for early collection. This to one is an easy way to scare the break minded and to gain easy access to your dear fortune ~ but it also spells cleverness and intelligence on their part. But take the case of this department. No thieves used any instrument to find their way into this well protected government owned house to steal. No, the locks were carefully opened and property worth about 3 million is at large.

"This town and the people inside it beat me and they interest me. Did your good dear mother fail to tell you that a friend to your enemy is also your enemy? If no, then take hint now and do not . be a fool like this K. Town man who nearly lost his dear life by making friendship to his enemy's friend. The simple thing about these people in this so-so tanap town is that all their talks are only about cash. Cash and nothing else. No matter where it comes from. They so have money that any time one is offering me a drink I have the unholy feeling that I am being sold to Nyongo. When I overheard this Fiango woman who recently closed her drinking house discuss business with a friend of mine my blood ran two percent below normal , nothing but purely cut throat methods, but I have one consolation when I aw in Kumba I trust the men more than the women. The other day a baby shaped like sin was delivered by one of my soldiers. When she was questioned how a handsome father like this car owner opposite this big market could produce such an image, she reported angrily', you no sabi say pikin fit fiber some man for your family? But has any of them such bent things that look like a sugar cane? The truth is that this my sister had been put in the way by a leper for cash sake. Na so-so tanap town this. "The public image of a rich man is often unfair but it can be doubly so in the case of a rich man who does not earn his own money, when I tell you that to have lots of money is not working twenty-four hours a day you might begin to wonder. A few brain, risky moves and there you are. Did you know how he acquired this wealth? He spent nothing. Really nothing but he owns a large College and is changing cars daily. There are three ways you can make early cash - beg, borrow or steal. The boys have been using these methods and succeeding.

"But when you ask them how they acquire their wealth they will tell you how they suffered. But the real secret is first what I have told you. "In the good old days you could leave your wife with a friend and go abroad to study on return you would find her as normal as good as you left her. That is when decent men existed. But not today. Take the case of this wealthy care-taker whose friend left his wife with him. He even helped finance his passage to Europe but hardly had the plane even taken off from Douala, tften he took her to bed and she is married to him, how she is so beautiful now that I have cough. Some of you do not even care to ask about my health. I made a mistake when travelling to Mamfe a few days ago.

"I had forgotten the state of the road. Dear, you need a special dust proof suit. Yesterday I remembered the story my dear mama always told me when I cried if I was given food without meat; Any time I think of this real story, I control my long throat.'

'The story is popular but I must tell you exactly how she saw it been in this. New year you must not carry your 'long throat' into 1979. Once they lived a man at Mbonge. This man was a member in all juju in the clan. Being this he had plenty of beef from new members. But once in a while members were not always around and thus no meat. So one day when his wife brought him plantains and pepper, he felt it was an insult. He took the moslem shaving knife, went behind the house, and cut his throat.

"I want you all to send me small dash. Don't you think if I were in Yaounde I would make about I ok before January 1979 goes out from dash. New year new fashion."

"SATURDAY JAN. 27, 1979; DECREE N9265

"In view of what happened during the Christmas and New Year. I Thomas Ako-Aya Commander of the Armed forces of Church Street Victoria and Hausa Quarters Kumba, Abakwa, Bamenda, Nkanne, Douala and Yaounde do decree as follows:

"This Order may be cited as the New Year Corruption Prevention Order.
"No one, corporate body or legal body should give New Year presents, New Year good wishes to any person except to the one person I may direct from year to year.

"Goats from Bamenda, Yams from Muyuka, Plantains from Kumba and fish from Fako that usually accompany such New Year presents and wishes should stop immediately. Money which usually accompanies such gifts should not be given let alone accepted.

"Persons breaking this decree will be dealt with seriously by my armed forces.

"This decree will be published in the Cameroon Outlook only and will come into force on the day of publication.

"FRIDAY MARCH 9, 1979:
KONTRY FASHION FOR PAMDA"

"All things become old and everything dong new, I forget this morning whether I am quoting from the Bible or from Plato, but what has surprised me most is the way the same thing takes different dimensions in different places.

"For Yawinde where I have been for the past week contractors no longer use the 20% to build houses for those who enabled them get the contract that is too old fashioned.

"A t the women t you are merely given an account number in a bank in France and asked to transfer the money there. In Bamenda even though Gov't is taking all steps to curb bribery and corruption but, to the dismay of the people, the addicts of bribery and corruption in Pamda have coined out a new word for it here to go safe. The word commonly used is 'country fashion.' "It was an embarrassment to me the other day to see some hardened prostitutes nicknamed their friends that you are the prostitutes with no tails - what was discovered later on to be the meaning is that these are prostitutes who can't measure up with the prostitutes that have throughout their life existed as prostitutes by profession.

"After visiting the West Coast of Victoria recently I have come to the understanding that B.A. Kwe people have a propensity for selling land. Their forebearers sold land to the German for stock fish and the present generation is also itching to sell its own land too. Have you seen

where a family man sells his house for shidishi?
Yet they ask shidishi for more land only of course to
sell it. Perhaps something could be done."

'WEDNESDAY MARCH 21, 1979:
MY FOOLISH DREAMS AGAIN"

"Bribery and corruption, awuf, country fashion cadeaux all these words I live with them daily that I wonder whether they mean anything more. "It is merely the system of things and if you live with the system it does not oppress you. How my dreams have tormented me so much about the above words that malaria has set in. I am considering going once again to Oku to cure myself. "Take the dream I had last week for instance. I became a very big doctor in charge of several hospitals. Then I was given 20 million francs to equip them - buy new blankets, bedsheets, pillows etc., just like Nguti St. John of God's Hospital is.

"I gave the contrary to my sister in-law and instructed her to supply nothing but to bring an invoice which she faithfully did. But a little girl insisted she must see the things before payment. I reported her to the police who threatened her with arrest but she remained unshakable. What surprised me was how a high -up P'c' could agree to be party to such things, well it is all chop I chop.

"Just like the other day a man working in a Butchery stole more than 50 kilos of meat. The man is very tiny, but from the first day he started working in the butchery he tied several rags of cloth round his stomach to give the impression say nyi belle big. At break time the rolls of cloth are removed and replaced with frozen beef.

"By one in the afternoon, he stepped into a side-walk where 3 P.c's were waiting for him. Dem buy beef for five kilos for one thousand. Soon the man had got 10.000 and replaced his stomach with the rags.

Chapter Twenty: Ako-Aya's Last Few Months on Earth

"So for this big Doctor in the end I was found out, removed from the big post and just now I am on transfer to Diwala."

Very few people in Victoria will ever efface the date, Sunday April 29th, 1979, when the news of Patrick Tataw Obenson's (alias Ako-Aya) death was made public. It sounded so unreal and yet it was for real; it appeared to be very impossible and yet it was possible; indeed, it sounded so untrue and yet it was all true - Ako-Aya was very dead.

Almost everyone on hearing the news must have reached out to his table and collected a copy of the previous day's paper, Cameroon Outlook, Saturday April 28th, 1979. So a few hours before his death Ako-Aya was still up and doing as seen in his last article dated April 28, 1979:

"FOR WAKA FOR PUT CATHOLIC D.O. DEM

"Do not blame me this morning for the revelations I will bring to you. Have you met this new Director of an Employment Agency, well I hear say him bureau dey for motor park. He does not advertise his vacancies and in any case all his jobs go only to girls and he gets them from mile Four, Bututu, Socolo in fact all the villages around Victoria.

"Before a girl is employed the Director must sign the employment form dipping his pen in Blue ink in order to sign. Thereafter the new employees are thrown to the mercy of Taxi drivers. Of the fourteen, ten are already pregnant and soon these will be put aside and the process repeats itself again.

"'You are a stranger in Bamenda', I overheard two people quarrelling. Both of them are from the West except that one is from the South and the other from the North. So how can a person be a stranger in his own country asked the other.

"The quarrel continued and I heard words leke 'Nkwa' and I was horrified. Down here, in Douala and Yaounde all of us are brothers but up there the stranger elements begins. Even the PWD Bamenda team is a 'stranger' team and has very little support, the only team which is most known is Mankon United.

"I was up to witness the installation of six Catholic D.O. 's and by five in the morning the Off-licences were full, "Ako-Aya we dong broke the law' one told me this na we own coffee for this morning. What could I say, they too have been caught by the system that, laws are only enforced for 24 hours, thereafter you can do what you please.
'Whilst up several women asked me that they heard Fotolia dong wake-up and that money dong come plenty. This has been so because some newspapers engage in exaggeration. As so many of them are preparing to come down I di warn dern say they may not have places to stay because Church Street dong flop.

"But you must see the new ticket office built in Bamenda Park. Just one old zinc like places where pigs are kept. Pamda na show-piece for Noriway - it ought to build better houses as ticket offices."

Chapter Twenty: Ako-Aya's Last Few Months on Earth

Picture Shows the Body of Mr. Obensen Lying in State in his Victoria Residence

Picture Shows the Crowd that Gathered to Pay their Last Respects

Epilogue

For true, Patrick Tataw Obenson, the rabid critic, social crusader and witty journalist, all rolled up in one, was indeed a man of the people. Little wonder that when he died, he left behind countless painful hearts and many questions on the lips of his admirers. As a man of the people, the fallen hero of Cameroon's Fleet Street shared his experiences, be they good or bad, with his readers. He was a virile critic even of the sordid things in which he himself secretly indulged. The promiscuous things that Tataw Obenson did behind the scene always provided rich stuff for his subsequent "Ako-Aya" column. Thus when he engaged the services of a prostitute and failed to settle the score by morning, because his pockets were more often than not lean, it was most likely to constitute part of the menu for the subsequent "Ako-Aya" column. Obenson's mind was open. In fact, the whole society could see through him, for, he virtually exposed its contents.

Only Tataw Obenson could spit out really scathing pieces of satire, aimed directly at the highest governing authorities of his society. Only Obenson could make allusions even to his own apparently ugly self. Only he could be liberal and honest enough to confess how he boarded a taxi and later bolted without paying the driver. Only Obenson was able to foresee his imminent demise from the face of the earth and literarily wrote his own epitaph.

But like all mortals, Patrick Tataw Obenson had his own fair share of human weakness. With all his intelligence, wit and avowed sense of perception, Obenson still fell victim to superstition, which he would otherwise have criticised like a re-incarnation of Christ the Lord? What with his own pilgrimages to Oku where the very people he lampooned also went to fortify themselves with amulets and talismans? What with tacitly subscribing to witchcraft and staying under the sun four hours daily, for five days in the belief that he would be cured of his ailment?

Yet, once more, only the lion-hearted and transparently frank Obenson could dare challenge his own doctors publicly, more so the much revered native doctors who are believed to hold people's lives in trust for them by some remote means. Whereas other journalists would easily submit to the whims and caprices of the affluent to benefit from some of their wealth, Obenson instead elected to beg openly even from people he had openly castigated before, and was still likely to castigate even after receiving their gifts.

In spite of his shabby appearance, and lean pockets, accentuated by poor proceeds from his newspapering, and the near inhuman conditions under which he operated, Obenson's vision remained clear and unbiased.

He had an axe to grind with all perpetrators of social vices, especially those of them that infringed on the rights of the common man. He gave them a good fight, using his newspaper as his only weapon - a weapon which could not be neutralized even by the most affluent nor the most coercive leadership. And he did so with nerve and valour and venom which is the handmaiden of the practice of journalism in better democracies.

Obenson had a style of his own. Thus, while his conge-neers were compelled to falsify events and sing the chorus of power-brokers and power-mongers and publicity addicts, under the guise that he who pays the piper dictates the tune, Obenson, on the contrary, was a thorn in their flesh, always rattling the skeletons in the cupboards of the morally bankrupt. He never jettisoned his professional code of conduct. He never lied to please certain individuals, interest groups or even his own self. He never passed as a bloody mercenary or as a mere cypher on the country's' political chessboard like most of his colleagues of the same profession. ... That was Patrick Tataw Obenson as I knew him. I wonder when and if this nation will ever be blessed with another him...

Titles by *Langaa* RPCIG

Francis B. Nyamnjoh
Stories from Abakwa
Mind Searching
The Disillusioned African
The Convert
Souls Forgotten
Married But Available
Intimate Strangers

Dibussi Tande
No Turning Back: Poems of Freedom 1990-1993
Scribbles from the Den: Essays on Politics and Collective Memory in Cameroon

Kangsen Feka Wakai
Fragmented Melodies

Ntemfac Ofege
Namondo, Child of the Water Spirits
Hot Water for the Famous Seven

Emmanuel Fru Doh
Not Yet Damascus
The Fire Within
Africa's Political Wastelands: The Bastardization of Cameroon
Oriki'badan
Wading the Tide
Stereotyping Africa: Surprising Answers to Surprising Questions

Thomas Jing
Tale of an African Woman

Peter Wuteh Vakunta
Grassfields Stories from Cameroon
Green Rape: Poetry for the Environment
Majunga Tok: Poems in Pidgin English
Cry, My Beloved Africa
No Love Lost
Straddling The Mungo: A Book of Poems in English & French

Ba'bila Mutia
Coils of Mortal Flesh

Kehbuma Langmia
Titabet and the Takumbeng
An Evil Meal of Evil
The Earth Mother

Victor Elame Musinga
The Bam
The Tragedy of Mr. No Balance

Ngessimo Mathe Mutaka
Building Capacity: Using TEFL and African Languages as Development-oriented Literacy Tools

Milton Krieger
Cameroon's Social Democratic Front: Its History and Prospects as an Opposition Political Party, 1990-2011

Sammy Oke Akombi
The Raped Amulet
The Woman Who Ate Python
Beware the Drives: Book of Verse
The Wages of Corruption

Susan Nkwentie Nde
Precipice
Second Engagement

Francis B. Nyamnjoh & Richard Fonteh Akum
The Cameroon GCE Crisis: A Test of Anglophone Solidarity

Joyce Ashuntantang & Dibussi Tande
Their Champagne Party Will End! Poems in Honor of Bate Besong

Emmanuel Achu
Disturbing the Peace

Rosemary Ekosso
The House of Falling Women

Peterkins Manyong
God the Politician

George Ngwane
The Power in the Writer: Collected Essays on Culture, Democracy & Development in Africa

John Percival
The 1961 Cameroon Plebiscite: Choice or Betrayal

Albert Azeyeh
Réussite scolaire, faillite sociale : généalogie mentale de la crise de l'Afrique noire francophone

Aloysius Ajab Amin & Jean-Luc Dubois
Croissance et développement au Cameroun : d'une croissance équilibrée à un développement équitable

Carlson Anyangwe
Imperialistic Politics in Cameroun:
Resistance & the Inception of the Restoration of the Statehood of Southern Cameroons
Betrayal of Too Trusting a People: The UN, the UK and the Trust Territory of the Southen Cameroons

Bill F. Ndi
K'Cracy, Trees in the Storm and Other Poems
Map: Musings On Ars Poetica
Thomas Lurting: The Fighting Sailor Turn'd Peaceable / Le marin combattant devenu paisible
Soleil et ombre

Kathryn Toure, Therese Mungah Shalo Tchombe & Thierry Karsenti
ICT and Changing Mindsets in Education

Charles Alobwed'Epie
The Day God Blinked
The Bad Samaritan
The Lady with the Sting

G. D. Nyamndi
Babi Yar Symphony
Whether losing, Whether winning
Tussles: Collected Plays
Dogs in the Sun

Samuel Ebelle Kingue
Si Dieu était tout un chacun de nous ?

Ignasio Malizani Jimu
Urban Appropriation and Transformation: bicycle, taxi and handcart operators in Mzuzu, Malawi

Justice Nyo' Wakai
Under the Broken Scale of Justice: The Law and My Times

John Eyong Mengot
A Pact of Ages

Ignasio Malizani Jimu
Urban Appropriation and Transformation: Bicycle Taxi and Handcart Operators

Joyce B. Ashuntantang
Landscaping and Coloniality: The Dissemination of Cameroon Anglophone Literature
I Cry When It's Cold

Jude Fokwang
Mediating Legitimacy: Chieftaincy and Democratisation in Two African Chiefdoms

Michael A. Yanou
Dispossession and Access to Land in South Africa: an African Perspevctive

Tikum Mbah Azonga
Cup Man and Other Stories
The Wooden Bicycle and Other Stories

John Nkemngong Nkengasong
Letters to Marions (And the Coming Generations)
The Call of Blood

Amady Aly Dieng
Les étudiants africains et la littérature négro-africaine d'expression française

Tah Asongwed
Born to Rule: Autobiography of a life President
Child of Earth

Frida Menkan Mbunda
Shadows From The Abyss

Bongasu Tanla Kishani
A Basket of Kola Nuts
Konglanjo (Spears of Love without Ill-fortune) and Letters to Ethiopia with some Random Poems

Fo Angwafo III S.A.N of Mankon
Royalty and Politics: The Story of My Life

Basil Diki
The Lord of Anomy
Shrouded Blessings

Churchill Ewumbue-Monono
Youth and Nation-Building in Cameroon: A Study of National Youth Day Messages and Leadership Discourse (1949-2009)

Emmanuel N. Chia, Joseph C. Suh & Alexandre Ndeffo Tene
Perspectives on Translation and Interpretation in Cameroon

Linus T. Asong
The Crown of Thorns
No Way to Die
A Legend of the Dead: Sequel of *The Crown of Thorns*
The Akroma File
Salvation Colony: Sequel to *No Way to Die*
Chopchair
Doctor Frederick Ngenito

Vivian Sihshu Yenika
Imitation Whiteman
Press Lake Varsity Girls: The Freshman Year

Beatrice Fri Bime
Someplace, Somewhere
Mystique: A Collection of Lake Myths

Shadrach A. Ambanasom
Son of the Native Soil
The Cameroonian Novel of English Expression: An Introduction
Education of the Deprived: Anglophone Cameroon Literary Drama
Homage and Courtship *(Romantic Stirrings of a Young Man)*

Tangie Nsoh Fonchingong and Gemandze John Bobuin
Cameroon: The Stakes and Challenges of Governance and Development

Tatah Mentan
Democratizing or Reconfiguring Predatory Autocracy? Myths and Realities in Africa Today

Roselyne M. Jua & Bate Besong
To the Budding Creative Writer: A Handbook

Albert Mukong
Prisonner without a Crime: Disciplining Dissent in Ahidjo's Cameroon

Mbuh Tennu Mbuh
In the Shadow of my Country

Bernard Nsokika Fonlon
Genuine Intellectuals: Academic and Social Responsibilities of Universities in Africa

Lilian Lem Atanga
Gender, Discourse and Power in the Cameroonian Parliament

Cornelius Mbifung Lambi & Emmanuel Neba Ndenecho
Ecology and Natural Resource Development in the Western Highlands of Cameroon: Issues in Natural Resource Managment

Gideon F. For-mukwai
Facing Adversity with Audacity

Peter W. Vakunta & Bill F. Ndi
Nul n'a le monopole du français : deux poètes du Cameroun anglophone

Emmanuel Matateyou
Les murmures de l'harmattan

Ekpe Inyang
The Hill Barbers

JK Bannavti
Rock of God *(Kilán ke Nyúy)*

Godfrey B. Tangwa (Rotcod Gobata)
I Spit on their Graves: Testimony Relevant to the Democratization Struggle in Cameroon

Henrietta Mambo Nyamnjoh
"We Get Nothing from Fishishing", Fishing for Boat Opportunies amongst Senegalese Fisher Migrants

Bill F. Ndi, Dieurat Clervoyant & Peter W. Vakunta
Les douleurs de la plume noire : du Cameroun anglophone à Haïti

Laurence Juma
Kileleshwa: A Tale of Love, Betrayal and Corruption in Kenya

Nol Alembong
Forest Echoes (Poems)

Marie-Hélène Mottin-Sylla & Joëlle Palmieri
Excision : les jeunes changent l'Afriaque par le TIC

Walter Gam Nkwi
Voicing the Voiceless: Contributions to Closing Gaps in Cameroon History, 1958-2009

John Koyela Fokwang
A Dictionary of Popular Bali Names

Alain-Joseph Sissao
(Translated from the French by Nina Tanti)
Folktales from the Moose of Burkina Faso

Ephraim N. Ngwafor
Ako-Aya: A Cameroonian Pioneer in Daring Journalism and Social Commentary

www.ingramcontent.com/pod-product-compliance
Lightning Source LLC
Chambersburg PA
CBHW011139290426
44108CB00020B/2687